The Framework: The Fluff-Free Guide to Understanding, Transforming and Reducing Stress, Autostress and Anxiety

Rebecca Marks

The Framework: The Fluff-Free Guide to Understanding, Transforming and
Reducing Stress, Autostress and Anxiety by Rebecca Marks
First Edition

Disclaimer:

This book is not intended to be a substitute for the medical advice of a licensed
physician. The information provided in this book is designed to provide helpful
information on the subjects discussed. This book is not meant to be used, nor should
it be used, to diagnose or treat any mental health condition. The reader should
consult with their doctor in any matters relating to his/her mental health. The author
is not responsible for any specific health needs that may require medical supervision
and is not liable for any damages or negative consequences from any treatment,
action, application or preparation, to any person reading or following the information
in this book. References are provided for informational purposes only and do not
constitute endorsement of any websites or other sources. Readers should be aware
that the websites listed in this book may change. The author admits that this book is
not in fact 'fluff-free' as claimed on the front cover. This book contains many cats.
Cats are fluffy. Therefore, this book actually contains a lot of fluff. It is 'fluff-full'.
Sorry.

ISBN 978 1 97704 526 3

Illustrations by Laura Tubb
www.lauratubb.co.uk

Edited by Daniel John
daniellewisjohn@gmail.com

*For everybody who feels lost and confused
because of anxiety and stress.*

CONTENTS

PART ONE: Situation

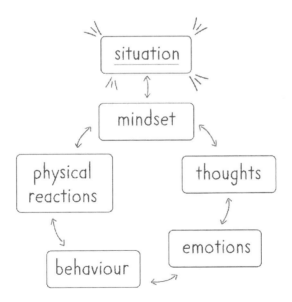

PART ONE: SITUATION
1: Introduction

We've all heard of the phrase "mind over matter". It can be defined as:

— *A situation in which someone is able to control a physical condition, problem, etc., by using the mind.*

In The Framework, we're going to explain how to use mind over matter.

We'll discover the amazing interconnectedness of our minds and bodies, and we'll learn how we can use this to our advantage.

To be more specific: we'll be explaining how we can use our mindsets, thoughts, and behaviour to change our emotions and physical reactions, so we can become calmer and happier.

To do this, we'll be taking you on a journey through the cognitive behavioural cycle, a.k.a. the CBT cycle. The CBT cycle is an extremely useful tool for understanding human psychology. Here's what it looks like:

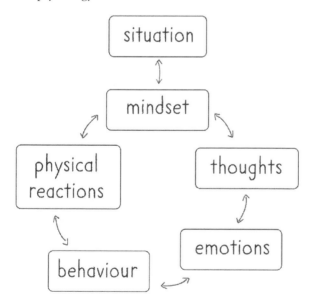

As you can see, the cycle demonstrates how our mindsets, thoughts, emotions, behavior and physical reactions are all interconnected. Each aspect of our life influences the others.

Without an understanding of the CBT cycle, it's easy to feel overwhelmed and unsure where to start when it comes to helping ourselves feel calmer and happier. And the struggle is extremely common—the Mental Health Foundation have found that 70% of women and young adults aged 18-34 in the UK have experienced a mental health difficulty.

When we invest time reflecting on different parts of our cycle, it gives us plenty of opportunities to make changes. As you'll discover, there are many small changes we can make to help alleviate stress, autostress and anxiety in our daily lives. Changing just one part of our cycle can make changing the other parts easier. Small steps create big changes.

To help you understand the CBT cycle, we'll be telling you the story of a woman called Polly. Let's start with her situation:

Polly is a 25-year-old support worker for people with severe and enduring mental health issues such as schizophrenia and bipolar disorder. Growing up, she got on fairly well with her Mum, but she had a difficult relationship with her Dad. As a child, she remembers being very scared of him. Her Dad never really spoke to her unless he was shouting, and he never seemed to take an interest in getting to know her or spending time with the family.

Needless to say, she was very happy to move away from home. Unfortunately, Polly also had a tough time at university. She studied at a top-ranking university and was surrounded by very wealthy people. Coming from a working-class family, she felt out of place, like she didn't belong. Throughout university she felt low and lonely and when around new people she felt very shy. She had a range of unpleasant physical symptoms that she'd learned to live with and came to view as a normal part of everyday life. She buried herself in her studies—she'd always been incredibly driven and hard-working, putting a lot of pressure on herself to do well.

Polly never went to the GP or told anyone about how bad she felt, although she did once go to an appointment at her university's counselling service. She found talking about her issues made her feel even worse, and she left feeling deflated.

Her mental and physical distress continued into her current job. Her typical work day often involves responding to people with suicidal thoughts and those about to be made homeless, all whilst keeping on top of mountains of paperwork.

Fortunately, since starting her new role, Polly has made some new friends that she's been able to start opening up to. They're all very interested in wellbeing and are pursuing careers in the field of clinical psychology. She joined a book club they set up, and over the past 2 years she's read and discussed these three books:

1. *Rewire Your Anxious Brain* by Catherine Pittman and Elizabeth Karle,
2. *The Happiness Trap* by Dr Russ Harris,
3. *The Upside of Stress* by Kelly McGonigal.

Applying the knowledge from these books along with the support of her new friendship group has resulted in her wellbeing gradually improving over the past two years. Now, she has a deep understanding of her mental health. She's successfully transforming and reducing her stress, autostress and anxiety, and for the first time in her life, she feels happy.

Let's learn how Polly did it, and how you can too.

PART TWO: Mindset
with Negative Nancy & Running Ruth

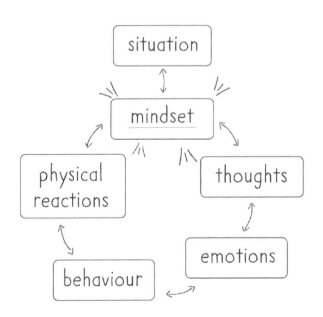

PART TWO: MINDSET
2.1: Different Methods Are Needed to Address Stress, Autostress and Anxiety

"Problems cannot be solved with the same mindset that created them." – Albert Einstein.

Our mindset refers to our *sets of beliefs about the world.*

We can think of them as our *core beliefs.* These beliefs shape our reality. They influence how we interpret the world, what we pay attention to, and ultimately, how we feel. Developing awareness of our mindsets is therefore an incredibly powerful tool when it comes to enhancing our wellbeing.

To access a core belief, we can keep asking ourselves 'why?'. This is called Socratic questioning, or the downward arrow technique. Here's an example:

I'll never feel better.
Why?
I've tried different things to help me feel less anxious and none of them have helped.
Why?
I'm an anxious person and there's nothing I can do about it.
Why?
Because of my genes. Anxiety runs in my family.
Why?
Because... anxiety is a genetic condition and science tells us there's nothing we can do about our genes.

Here, the core belief is about how anxiety is genetic and therefore incurable. And this core belief is false. It's true that we can be born with a vulnerability towards stress and anxiety, but new scientific research in this area is incredibly empowering. We truly have the power to rewire our brains and calm our bodies.

In this part of The Framework, we'll take a look at three of Polly's new mindsets that are influencing her CBT cycle in ways that are helping her alleviate stress, autostress and anxiety.

Her first new mindset is: different methods are needed to address stress, autostress and anxiety. Before, stress and anxiety were fuzzy terms that she used interchangeably. After reading about them, she now understands what they are, how they affect her, and what she can do about it.

So, what exactly are stress, autostress and anxiety? Their exact definitions have actually been a subject of debate by experts for a long time.

Stress

Kelly McGonigal, an expert in the new science of stress, offers us this definition: *"stress is what arises when something we care about is at stake".*

Stress is best understood as manifesting in the body. It's the racing heart, sweaty palms and funny tummy we're all familiar with. A key part in all this stress is the amygdala, the part of the brain responsible for generating our stress response.

Experts agree that central to the definition of stress is the perception of threat and danger. You've probably heard of the 'fight-or-flight' stress response as a reaction to perceived danger. In fact, we have various stress responses. For example, we experience a different type of stress response when we perceive a challenge. It's possible to transform our stress response in a way which helps us perform. As we'll discover, our beliefs about stress and our mindset play an important part in how it impacts us.

Autostress

Dr John Arden, author of several books integrating neuroscience and psychotherapy, recently put forward the term *autostress* for describing what happens when our body's stress response goes on for a long time. He explains:

> *"Like autoimmune disorders that hijack the immune system, attacking the body instead of protecting it, autostress [transforms] the stress response system into something that attacks the self rather than protecting it."*

When we're autostressed, we experience a wide range of physical stress symptoms on an ongoing basis, such as breathing difficulties, heart palpitations, chest tightness, headaches, IBS, light-headedness, and so forth. We experience these symptoms regardless of our situation.

Autostress is associated with what psychologists call a high level of *stress reactivity*. People with high levels of stress reactivity may be more vulnerable to developing autostress. They may release more stress hormones, have a stronger sympathetic nervous system reaction, experience higher blood pressure, and/or have a higher heart rate during their stress response. Throughout their lives, people with high stress reactivity may experience stress responses that feel out of proportion to the situation. Anxiety is currently conceptualised as encompassing both mental and physical symptoms. In The Framework, I'm arguing that autostress is a better term for understanding the physical symptoms of anxiety. I feel the term autostress yields more understanding and more compassion. I believe the distinction is particularly important as different methods are needed to address physical symptoms (what I label autostress) and mental symptoms (what I label anxiety).

Anxiety

Polly's thoughts on a bus: "I feel dizzy and light-headed... What if I faint?"

Polly's thoughts in bed: "Why can't I sleep?! My presentation tomorrow is going to be so bad. Oh God, it's going to be so embarrassing if my mind goes blank and I forget what I'm saying. Catherine will regret promoting me. If I'm demoted I won't be able to afford to keep up with my higher rent. Arghhh.. What if I don't get any sleep at all?"

*Polly's thoughts on a night out: "Erghhh.. My heart is beating so fast all of a sudden. This is horrible. I'm so sick of this. [*Imagines having a panic attack in the middle of the dance floor*]"*

This is anxiety—the unhelpful thinking patterns we experience when our thoughts and mental images zoom in on horrible possible outcomes and negative aspects of situations. Anxiety is common in creative people, as their creativity gives them the ability to imagine a wide array of potentially frightening scenarios. Anxiety is something that easily spirals out of control, and as such, easily affects our mood. Along with anxious thoughts, people experiencing anxiety might also feel a sense of impending doom: feeling apprehensive, fearful, and constantly on edge, even at times when there is no immediate threat.

We're more vulnerable to anxiety when we've grown up with parents or caregivers who were overly attentive to danger and threats. This can lead us to having a mentality that the world isn't a safe place.

Anxiety can occur on its own, as a response to stress, or it can trigger stress. When it occurs as a response to stress, it can intensify our stress response, creating a stress-anxiety loop. In worst cases, this can lead to panic attacks.

Anxiety comes from an area called the prefrontal-cortex, located at the very front of our brain.

We have more power over our anxiety than we have over our body's stress response. This is because our amygdala—the part of our brain that triggers the stress response—is extremely powerful. It can even operate on a subconscious level, which is why we can often feel out of control and confused in moments of high stress.

It might help you to think of stress, autostress and anxiety as two living beings inside our heads: Running Ruth and Negative Nancy.

Stress and Autostress: Our Inner Running Ruth

You feel your heart beating faster and stronger, your breathing becomes shallower, and your palms start to sweat. This is when you can imagine your inner Running Ruth arriving. Why running? Because we feel like we're out for a run even if we're lying in bed.

Running Ruth

Our inner Running Ruth helps us rise to challenges and deal with threats by altering our bodily responses. She pumps more blood to our brains by making our hearts beat faster, which helps our cognitive performance. She boosts our energy levels by releasing cortisol and helps us focus better by releasing adrenaline.

If your Running Ruth has been busy from a young age, she's more likely to be stronger and more active in adulthood. For those with autostress, she's so active that she'll go running for no reason, usually at really inconvenient times. To help ourselves feel calmer, we need to learn how to give her a rest!

Anxiety: Our Inner Negative Nancy

Negative Nancy hijacks our mind with negative thoughts and worries she wants us to pay attention to. She does this because she thinks she's being helpful. To be fair to her, she was helpful. 70,000 years ago, she was very helpful. Today, not so much. Whilst it was important for our ancient ancestors to be on high alert for danger, it's not as important for us in the 21st century.

Negative Nancy

Hijacking us with negative thoughts and worries is a skill she develops over time—the more she's done it, the quicker and easier it gets for her.

To help ourselves feel calmer, we need to learn how to reduce the impact of what she tells us, so that she doesn't spend so long hijacking our minds.

Just like some people have a stronger Running Ruth, some people have a louder Negative Nancy. In people who experience problematic anxiety, their unhelpful thinking patterns are more prominent, more difficult to control, and excessive given the situation.

SUMMARY 2.1

I hope you'll have started adopting your first new mindset: different methods are needed to address stress, autostress and anxiety.

Broadly speaking, we're aiming to:

- Transform stress,
- Reduce autostress and anxiety.

And it's complex: different methods work at different times for different people. It's a skill, and some of us need to work harder at it than others.

Ultimately, what we need to do is become the scientists of our own wellbeing, trying and testing different methods in order to discover what works best for us. Investing time in understanding and enhancing our wellbeing is one of the best investments we could ever make.

I mentioned earlier that our body's stress response is different depending on whether we see our situation as a challenge or as a threat. In the next section, we'll learn how we can transform our stress response from the threat response into the challenge response.

2.2: It's Possible to Transform Our Body's Stress Response

"When you choose to view your stress response as helpful, you create the biology of courage." – Kelly McGonigal

After reading Kelly McGonigal's book The Upside of Stress, Polly was surprised to find that her core beliefs about stress were fundamentally flawed.

She used to think that stress was simply her body going into fight-or-flight mode, but she now understands that her stress response is more complicated, and a lot of it has to do with her mindset.

Welcome Science Cat! (When Science Cat arrives, that's when you know we're about to get down to some nerdy science.)

So, our body's stress response can actually activate several biological systems—not just the fight-or-flight response. Each system helps our minds and bodies cope with different types of challenging and threatening situations.

Jim Blascovich is a pioneer in this field. He's spent his career developing what he calls the *biopsychosocial model of challenge and threat.* The challenge and threat responses represent different ends of a physiological spectrum. Here's an overview:

threat response

Body preparing us for damage
(a.k.a. the 'fight or flight' response,
or the 'fight, flight or freeze response')

Influenced by negative mindsets and
anxiety which act as a danger
signal to the brain

Leads to constricted blood vessels
and less blood to the brain and muscles

Associated with poorer health
and performance

challenge response

Body preparing us for action

Influenced by positive mindsets
which act as a challenge signal
to the brain

Leads to relaxed blood vessels and
more blood to the brain and muscles

Associated with enhanced
health and performance

The threat response is what everyone knows as the classic flight-or-flight response, and it's our body's way of preparing us for damage. It happens when our brain detects danger or threat, which can be physical danger or social danger (for example, the fear of social rejection).

On the other hand, the challenge response is our body's way of preparing us for action. You might know a natural challenge responder. They're the people who say they feel 'pumped' instead of 'stressed'. What makes them different? Their mindset.

Positive mindsets are what shift us into the challenge response. When someone says they're pumped, it's likely they're focusing on the positives in the situation, such as potential gains and opportunities for growth. They still experience a stress response—their hearts beat stronger and faster, but their blood vessels remain relaxed.

When someone says they feel stressed, it's likely they're focusing on the negatives, such as worrying about possible negative outcomes or berating themselves with negative self-talk. A negative mindset can easily become a self-fulfilling prophecy. This is due to our physical reactions in the threat response—we're less likely to perform well because our blood vessels are more constricted, and less blood gets to our brain and muscles. If you've ever had a negative mindset and experienced brain freeze (for example, during public speaking or an exam), now you know why!

We can experience the threat response when we're overwhelmed with things to do, and when we put a lot of pressure on ourselves to do well. In these situations, we're signalling to our brains that our demands outweigh our resources. Our brains interpret this as danger, and we shift into the threat response.

This is typical of people who experience high-functioning anxiety. 'High-functioning' refers to people who feel they're doing well in their jobs and life in general but live with anxiety as part of their everyday lives. Nicky Lidbetter, CEO of Anxiety UK, explains:

> *"Individuals who experience high functioning anxiety are often very driven, high achievers who set incredibly high standards for themselves. They can find themselves constantly striving for perfection in everything they turn their hand to."*

Here's the good news: research shows we can shift into the challenge response just by adopting a positive mindset about stress itself. For example, a study in 2013 by Alia Crum and colleagues at Yale University showed that people made the shift from a threat response to a challenge response after watching just three 3-minute videos describing how our body's stress response can help us perform.

It's possible that understanding in better detail about the body's stress response made people more accepting of their physical reactions instead of fighting against them. Understanding and accepting their physical reactions therefore prevented the stress-anxiety loop of escalating stress and anxiety.

SUMMARY 2.2
Here's our second new mindset we hope you'll have started adopting: it's possible to transform our body's stress response.

Our stress response is more than just the fight-or-flight response. When we feel our body's stress response being triggered, our mindset matters.

Focusing on the negatives is like sending a 'danger' signal to our brain. This causes our bodies to react in a way that protects us from physical harm—our blood vessels constrict, and we get less blood to our brain and muscles. When this continues for a long time, we risk entering a state of autostress, where we experience stress symptoms on an ongoing basis.

On the other hand, focusing on the positives sends a 'challenge' signal to our brain. This causes our bodies to react in a way that prepares us for action—our heart still beats stronger and faster, but our blood vessels remain relaxed, whilst we get more blood to our brain and muscles.

pawsitivity is key

We'll get onto how we can adopt a more positive mindset about stress shortly. But first, what's the #1 mindset for reducing anxiety?

2.3: To Reduce Anxiety, We Must Notice Thoughts as Just Thoughts and Focus on Our Response

"Between stimulus and response there is a space. In that space is our power to choose our response. In our response lies our growth and our freedom." – Victor Frankl.

Freedom from anxiety begins with recognising that thoughts are just thoughts, and we have the power to choose our response to them.

Thinking is a habit, and just like eating habits, we all have thinking habits. Our thinking habits are the patterns our thoughts tend to follow in response to different situations. These patterns are shaped by our upbringing and our core beliefs about the world.

Recognising these patterns and the power we have when responding to them is key to reducing anxiety and becoming better at managing our emotions in general. When we don't recognise our power to respond, we become a slave to the thinking habits we've passively adopted. Our emotions, behaviour and physical reactions largely lie in the hands of these automatic thinking habits. It's time to start taking notice of them!

A useful analogy is the Slide of Doom. Our inner Negative Nancy—our anxiety—starts at the top of the slide when she tells us our first negative thought or worry. The more negative thoughts and worries she hijacks us with, the further she gets down the slide.

Slide of Doom

Our goal is to stop her getting to the bottom, which is when her hijacking of our minds has resulted in her hijacking our mood.

Practising meditation is an effective and popular way to become better at observing our thoughts. With her new meditation habit and cognitive techniques that we'll describe in 3.2, Polly can now spot Negative Nancy at the top of the slide, and now—more often than not—she can stop her getting to the bottom.

SUMMARY 2.3
Here's a recap of the three new mindsets we'd like to introduce:

> 1) Different methods are needed to address stress, autostress and anxiety,
> 2) It's possible to transform our body's stress response,
> 3) To reduce anxiety, we must notice thoughts as just thoughts, and focus on our response.

In the next section, we'll outline three of Polly's new thinking patterns that help her transform her stress response and reduce anxiety.

PART THREE: Thoughts

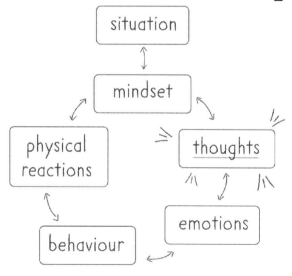

PART THREE: THOUGHTS
3.1: Three Thinking Patterns to Alleviate Stress, Autostress and Anxiety

"It hurt because it mattered." – John Green

With new mindsets, come new thinking patterns.

In the past, when Polly felt her body's stress response her thoughts focused on how unpleasant it was:

"This is horrible"
"I can't stand feeling like this"
"My heart's beating so fast, I think I'm starting to feel light-headed… what if I faint?"

Instead of fighting against her stress response, she's learning to accept it. Accepting our body's stress response can be the quickest way to feel calmer.

Everyone varies in their experience of the stress response. Here are some common physical reactions:

- Heart pounding and racing,
- Heart palpitations,
- Irregular heartbeat,
- Feeling dizzy and light-headed,
- Neck and shoulder tension,
- Clenched jaw,
- Grinding your teeth (especially at night),
- Headaches,
- General aches, pains and tense muscles,
- Shaking hands and legs,
- Breathing difficulties (for example, feeling as though you can't get enough air),
- Excessive yawning,
- Faster breathing,
- Chest tightness,
- Sweating or hot flushes,
- Pins and needles,
- IBS,
- Restlessness,
- Low energy,
- Ringing in the ear,

- Tingling or numbness in the arms, fingers, toes, or around the mouth,
- Fatigue,
- Feeling sick,
- Frequent urination,
- Changes in sex drive,
- Frequent colds,
- Feelings of unreality (of the self and the world).

Alongside these physical experiences, some people feel panicky for no reason. People might feel an ongoing sense of fear and impending doom. This can happen when the part of our brain that generates the stress response—the amygdala—becomes overactive and makes us hypervigilant to all possible threats in our environment. It makes our minds zoom in on the negative, which would have helped our ancient ancestors keep safe when they kept coming across life-threatening danger.

During the stress-anxiety loop, we might become extremely vigilant of our distressing physical symptoms and interpret them as being dangerous. When this happens, we risk experiencing escalating stress and anxiety that at worst, can result in a panic attack.

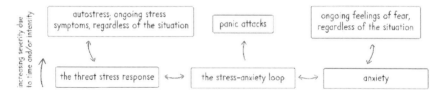

Key to overcoming this negative spiral is taking control of our minds. As Paulo Coelho says:

> *"You have two choices, to control your mind or to let your mind control you."*

With her new mindsets, Polly has three new thinking patterns helping her take control of her mind:

New Thinking Pattern 1: Focusing on the Benefits of Stress

To help us become more accepting of our body's stress response in moments of high stress, there are plenty of benefits we can focus on. Here are some examples of new thoughts:

'My heart's beating fast—that's good—I'm getting more blood to my brain, and it's helping my cognitive performance.'

'Adrenaline is helping me focus more and process information even quicker.'

'My energy levels are being boosted through cortisol increasing my blood sugar levels.'

'The neurosteroid DHEA is helping me become more resilient and learn from my experiences.'

'Oxytocin is encouraging me to get social support and it's helping my heart cells repair and regenerate.'

New Thinking Pattern 2: Focusing on The Meaning of Stress

Seeing the meaning in stress can shift us into a more positive, self-compassionate, and proactive mindset. The scientific research that lead to the mainstream view that stress is purely harmful was mainly done on mice experiencing the worst kind of stress possible: stress lacking any kind of meaning, as well as being unpredictable and uncontrollable. Whilst this kind of stress exists in extreme situations, most of the stress we experience on a daily basis we can in fact find meaning in, as well as anticipate and control.

Research shows that stress is strongly associated with finding life meaningful—it's an inevitable part of pursuing personal goals and caring about things important to us. Interestingly, finding life meaningful has also been associated with living longer. A study by Neal Krause in 2009 found that in a sample of 1,361 adults, people who felt their life was meaningful were less likely to die during the study than people who didn't have a strong sense of meaning. When it comes to focusing on the meaning of stress, here are three questions we can consider:

1) Which of My Personal Values Does It Relate To?

Studies show that reflecting on our personal values is in fact one of the most effective psychological interventions around. This insight helps Polly understand her stress response on a regular basis. It explained one of the strangest situations she found herself feeling stressed. In a conversation with a friend of a friend, the topic of conversation quickly shifted to something she was very interested in. All of a sudden, her heart started to beat quickly. At the time, she felt confused and annoyed at her body for reacting that way. She later remembered the experience and Kelly McGonigal's definition of stress: *"stress is what arises when something we care about is at stake"*. She realised that her amygdala, the part of her brain that generates the stress response, had detected something personally meaningful to her; it related to her value of social connection and meaningful conversations.

Another example is when she experiences stress often at work. When this happens, she knows it's because she cares about the wellbeing of the people she supports. She also cares greatly about her work performance. This puts her in a much more positive mindset by reminding her that she feels grateful for her job and cares a lot about it.

There's a flipside to this worth considering. Often, we get ourselves worked up over things which upon reflection, we might care less about than we originally thought. Sarah Knight, author of The Life-Changing Magic of Not Giving A F*ck, explains her experience:

> *"I stopped caring about small things that annoyed me. I unfriended some truly irritating people on Facebook. I refused to suffer through another reading of friends' plays. And I stopped getting dressed up just to go to the grocery store behind my house (pyjamas are the new black). Little by little, I started feeling better. Less burdened. More peaceful."*

Next time you feel stressed or anxious, you can ask yourself: how much does this really matter? Or as Sarah would say, should I actually give a f*ck? This applies to lots of common situations:

- Other people's opinions,
- People-pleasing,
- What we label our daily hassles,
- Our personal commitments,
- Situations where our perfectionism creeps in.

Letting go of caring so much about things that don't actually matter can be a simple and powerful way to feel calmer and happier!

2) Which Core Beliefs Does It Relate To?

The stress response can also be related to our core beliefs. For example, people who experience stress in social situations often hold the belief that they need social approval in order to feel worthy. Working on accepting ourselves and accepting that nobody appeals to everybody can help us overcome this kind of stress.

Jules Evans, an author who researches wellbeing, resilience and practical philosophy, talks about this in his book Philosophy for Life. He explains:

> *"I held certain toxic beliefs and habits of thinking which were poisoning me, such as [...] 'Everyone must approve of me, and if they don't, it's a disaster.' These toxic beliefs were at the core of my emotional suffering. My emotions followed my beliefs, and I would feel extremely anxious in social situations, and depressed when those situations did not go well."*

Another way our core beliefs can influence our stress response is in circumstances where they're out of sync with our behaviour. Psychologists call this 'cognitive dissonance'. For example, in her previous marketing job, Polly noticed her autostress flare up when she was working with a client whose business practises she didn't agree with.

3) Which Basic Needs Am I Not Meeting?

As humans, we all share the same basic needs that we must meet to have healthy minds and bodies, such as:

- A sense of safety and security,
- Enough rest and sleep,
- Sufficient exercise,
- Social connection,
- A healthy diet.

Polly, like a lot of us in the 21st century, struggles with getting enough rest. When she's been on the go too much and starts experiencing autostress, she knows it's her body telling her she needs to slow down and invest in rest. If she doesn't pay attention to these signs, she risks spiralling down into burnout zone.

When this happens, we can end up experiencing depression, where all our energy and desire to do anything disappears. This response can be seen as the body's way of hibernating in order to regain balance, and our brains way of removing us from what it perceives as a threatening situation. We'll be exploring more about the importance of meeting our basic needs in part five of The Framework.

New Thinking Pattern 3: Focus On 'Getting Excited'

Another way to transform our stress response and reduce anxiety is by simply telling ourselves to get excited!

This worked for a group of people that participated in a public speaking task in a study by Alison Brooks. In 2014 at Harvard Business School, Brooks found that people who told themselves "I am excited" compared to those who said "I am calm" ended up:

- Speaking for longer,
- Coming across more persistent,
- Being perceived as more persuasive, competent and confident.

SUMMARY 3.1

How about trying these new thinking patterns when you feel your body's stress response?

- Focusing on the benefits of stress,
  - Our hearts beat stronger and faster so that more blood gets to our brain, which can boost our cognitive performance.
  - Adrenaline can help us focus better and process information quicker.
  - Increased cortisol can help boost our energy levels.
  - The neurosteroid DHEA can help us become more resilient and learn from our experiences.
  - Oxytocin can encourage us to seek social support and it helps our heart cells repair and regenerate.
- Focusing on the meaning of stress:
  - Which of my personal values does it relate to?
  - How much does this really matter?
  - Which of my core beliefs does it relate to?
  - Which basic needs am I not meeting?
- Focusing on getting excited.

These thinking patterns can help us alleviate stress, autostress and anxiety by shifting us into the challenge response and signalling to us if there's anything we need to change in our lives.

Next, we'll describe five negative thinking habits to be aware of, and two important techniques—cognitive defusion and cognitive restructuring—to help us overcome them.

3.2: Cognitive Defusion and Cognitive Restructuring Techniques

"Most people don't realise that our mind constantly chatters. And yet, that chatter ends up being the force that drives us much of the day in terms of what we do, what we react to, and how we feel." – Jon Kabat-Zinn

We heard in 2.3 that the key to reducing anxiety is to notice thoughts as just thoughts and focus on our response. Once we get into the habit of noticing our thoughts, we'll eventually start noticing our thinking patterns. Here are some common unhelpful thinking patterns related to anxiety to be aware of:

1. **Hypothetical Worry**
Worry is normal and only becomes an unhelpful thinking habit when we focus too much on *hypothetical* worries instead of *practical* worries. Hypothetical worries include 'what if?' thoughts and are typically things we don't have control over. This type of worry is common in people who feel uncomfortable with the feeling of uncertainty. On the other hand, practical worries are things we can act on, and they can help us keep organised. Learning to distinguish between the two is key to overcoming anxiety.

2. **Rumination**
Rumination is when we repeatedly think about our bad experiences, dwelling on things that have distressed us, a.k.a., 'overthinking'. This unhelpful thinking habit becomes particularly problematic when we focus on the causes and consequences of distressing events instead of what we've learnt and would do differently in future.

3. **Catastrophising**
People who experience hypothetical worry and rumination may also be prone to catastrophising. This is when our thoughts jump to worst case scenarios, exaggerating the negatives, or as the saying goes, 'making a mountain out of a molehill'. People prone to catastrophising might notice their minds conjuring up mental images of worst case scenarios, which research shows tends to be more stress-inducing than thought-based anxiety.

4. **Pessimistic Thinking**
When our thoughts focus on the negatives and aren't balanced by acknowledging the good, we're experiencing pessimistic thinking; it's like our minds have put on a pair of Negativity Glasses which filter out anything positive. The glass is always half empty.

5. **Black-and-White Thinking**
When our thoughts centre on seeing situations and people in terms of extremes, labelling things as 'good' or 'bad', 'right' or 'wrong', 'perfect or 'imperfect', we're

experiencing black-and-white, or 'all or nothing' thinking. In reality, the world is full of shades of grey, and acknowledging these can play a big part in helping us reduce anxiety.

In Acceptance and Commitment Therapy (ACT, pronounced 'act' for short), when we're not aware of the space between our thoughts and our response to them, we're experiencing what's referred to as *cognitive fusion*.

In a state of cognitive fusion, we forget that our thoughts are just thoughts, we treat them as truth, and we fall deeper and deeper into downward spirals of negative emotions. In other words, our inner Negative Nancy always ends up at the bottom of the Slide of Doom; our thoughts always end up hijacking our mood.

Buddhist philosophy contains numerous helpful tips and metaphors for mental wellness. Here's one that helps explain this concept of cognitive fusion further.

In Buddhism, as well as the Western notion of five senses—sight, smell, hearing, taste, and touch—they have an additional sense, 'mind' or 'mental object'. Our minds are seen by Buddhists as a *sixth sense* that creates a filter on top of reality.

The Buddha taught that mental suffering arises from mistaking that filter for reality itself. Just as we can observe what we see, smell, hear, taste, and touch, we can also observe the activity of our mind.

When we're so fused to our thoughts that we can't take a step back and observe them as our mind's activity, we're in a state of cognitive fusion.

Meditation and *cognitive defusion techniques* train us to start observing our mind as we would observe a smell: as something to notice and respond to if we wish. A label you might find helpful for escaping cognitive fusion is thinking of your thoughts as 'brain noise'. This is an example of a cognitive defusion technique. These techniques help remind us that thoughts aren't facts and we can choose how to respond to them.

Two more examples of cognitive defusion techniques are:

- Saying "I'm having the thought that" before our unhelpful thoughts
- Imagining our thoughts being spoken in a silly voice by our inner Negative Nancy character

Another technique which is central to cognitive behavioural therapy (CBT) is to practise *cognitive restructuring*. For anxiety related to daily hassles (for example, delayed or cancelled trains), people often find cognitive defusion techniques most useful. On the other hand, when anxiety is related to our core beliefs (for example, our personal insecurities and negative self-talk), we might find cognitive restructuring to be more effective in the long run. Ultimately, everyone is different—remember, try and test—and discover what works best for you!

An example of cognitive restructuring is what we call the *BOP method* (you can bring to mind that toy from the 90's to help you remember!).

At the core of anxiety is focusing on and exaggerating the negative as well as focusing too much on hypothetical worries. To combat this, the BOP method trains our thinking habits to become more *balanced, optimistic* and *proactive*.

Balanced
In balanced thinking, we move away from pessimistic, black-and-white and catastrophic thinking by bringing to mind the wider, more realistic picture. We can ask ourselves:

- What assumptions am I making?
- What's the bigger picture?
- If I viewed this from an outsider perspective, what would I think?
- Will this matter in a week, a month or a year's time?
- Is this fact or opinion?

Optimistic
In optimistic thinking, we're rewiring our brains to become more *realistically* positive, which helps us combat anxiety as well as increasing our overall happiness levels.

Susan Jeffers, author of best-selling book Feel the Fear and Do It Anyway, suggests the following mantra that fits with optimistic thinking: *"whatever happens, I'll handle it."*

It's important to note that what we're aiming for isn't simply positive thinking, it's *realistic optimism*. Realistic optimism helps us see the good whilst still acknowledging the negatives.

We can ask ourselves:

- What are the positives, or potential positives, in this situation?
- Does the situation involve opportunities for growth, character development, or learning?
- What do I have to be grateful for right now?

Proactive

As well as consuming us with hypothetical worries, stress and anxiety can make us feel frozen and unable to take action. We feel an urge to withdraw and avoid what makes us feel stressed, even when it's something that matters to us. To let go of hypothetical worries and shift into a habit of more proactive thinking, we can ask ourselves:

- Is there something I need to let go of because I can't control it?
- What can I control in this situation?
- What's the smallest action I can take that could make a positive difference right now?

You might find the following mantra helpful: *"be proactive, not reactive."*

Research shows that when we shift our focus to what we can control, we see meaningful and lasting differences in our wellbeing, health, and performance.

We can use apps like Google Keep and Google Calendar to prevent us from feeling overwhelmed and to help keep us focused on proactivity. They can help us break down tasks into smaller steps, create to do lists and set reminders. This all helps us to keep on top of life's demands to our best ability.

We can also use these apps to try a technique suggested by Robert Leahy, author of The Worry Cure. He suggests making a note of our worries throughout the day, then reviewing them at the end of the day. He explains that most people who do this for a few weeks soon realise their worries are repetitive and unimportant, taking their power away from us.

Another form of proactive thinking is to focus on developing our problem-solving skills. When we're faced with an issue we can control, we can get into the habit of writing down exactly what the problem is, and all of the possible solutions we can think of. We then evaluate the solutions, choose one to try, and make a plan. If it doesn't work, we can come back to our notes and try something else. Typing up or writing out notes is a lot better than trying to problem-solve in our heads— everything becomes clearer when it's written down!

Cognitive Defusion and Restructuring in Action

Here's an example of how Polly uses cognitive defusion and the BOP method when faced with perceived social danger.

Polly opens up to a friend and tells her about her self-esteem issues. Her friend responds "you have so many great qualities you could focus on to build up your self-esteem. You're a great friend, hard-working, and caring. They're all qualities I really value in others". However, her friend pauses for a while before she says this. Uh oh! Polly's immediate response is anxiety:

> *"She took a long time to respond and looked uncomfortable (pessimistic thinking). She probably doesn't like me (catastrophising). What if she tells everyone what I told her? What if she starts thinking I'm a loser and stops inviting me to things? (hypothetical worry). This sucks —I really want her as a friend (anxiety starting to affect mood)."*

At this point, she notices she's stuck in cognitive fusion, treating her thoughts as absolute truths and spiralling further down the Slide of Doom. She then focuses her attention to cognitive defusion and cognitive restructuring:

> *"OK, I'm having the thought that she probably doesn't like me (cognitive defusion). Actually, I might be reading too much into it. Maybe she was thinking about what to say because she cares about me, or maybe she finds complimenting people a bit awkward, like me (balanced). What she said was actually really nice. And I agree, like she said, I am a good friend and I'm caring (optimistic). I'll take her advice and start focusing more on my positive qualities (proactive)."*

The more Polly practises cognitive defusion and cognitive restructuring, the more it becomes her natural way of thinking. She's taking control of her thinking habits and reshaping them to serve her better.

As I've mentioned, it's important to remember that thinking habits are just that, habits. Habits are difficult to break. When we spend years thinking in a certain way, it takes time and effort to change our way of thinking. We can think of getting mentally fit in the same way as we think of getting physically fit—it doesn't happen overnight, but with time and effort, it's totally possible!

bonus cat

Cognitive Distraction

In moments of high anxiety and racing thoughts, it might feel difficult to practise cognitive defusion and cognitive restructuring techniques. When we start practising methods for enhancing our wellbeing, we'll discover what tends to work best for us and when. It's like we develop our own personal response spectrum for what works best in times of mild, moderate and high distress. Cognitive distraction is something we might opt for in moments of high distress.

Distraction isn't about avoidance—it's a way of allowing our emotions to naturally defuse and our thoughts to quieten down, giving us the chance to make a more mindful decision about whatever it is we choose to do next.

Some ideas for cognitive distraction include:

- Watching something,
- Going for a walk,
- Listening to a podcast,
- Listening to music,
- Talking to someone,
- Counting backwards from 200 in 5s,
- Doing a grounding exercise (focusing on your senses, noticing what you can see, feel, smell, touch),
- A pampering activity such as painting your nails or doing a face mask,
- Writing in a journal,
- Cleaning or tidying,
- Practising other relaxation techniques, as we'll explore in section 5.2.

SUMMARY 3.2

Unhelpful thinking patterns create negative moods, put us at risk of negative self-fulfilling prophecies, and risk shifting us into the threat response. If our unhelpful thinking patterns continue long enough, they put us at risk of experiencing autostress.

Common unhelpful thinking patterns include:

- Hypothetical worry,
- Rumination,
- Catastrophising,
- Pessimistic thinking,
- Black-and-white thinking.

When we don't recognise our unhelpful thoughts hijacking our mood, we're in a state of cognitive fusion.

To combat cognitive fusion, we must notice thoughts as just thoughts, and focus on our response. To do this, we can start getting into the habit of using cognitive defusion, cognitive restructuring, and cognitive distraction techniques. These techniques help reduce the impact of negative thoughts and worries on the rest on our emotions, behaviour and physical reactions.

Examples of cognitive defusion is labelling our thoughts as 'brain noise', saying to ourselves "I'm having the thought that" before our thought, or imagining them being said in a silly voice.

An example of cognitive restructuring is the BOP method, which involves focusing our attention on balanced, optimistic and proactive thoughts.

balanced:	optimistic:	proactive:
what assumptions am I making?	what are the positives, or potential positives, in this situation?	is there something I need to let go of because I can't control it?
what's the bigger picture?	does the situation involve opportunities for growth, character development, or learning?	what can I control in this situation?
if I viewed this from an outsider perspective, what would I think?		what's the smallest action I can take that could make a positive difference right now?
will this matter in a week, a month, or a year's time?	what do I have to be grateful for right now?	
is this fact or opinion?		

Examples of cognitive distraction techniques include watching something, going for a walk, or listening to a podcast.

There are endless techniques to explore. It's all about finding what works best for you!

In the next section, we'll describe three important points about the psychology of emotion. When put into practise, these can help you boost your happiness levels.

PART FOUR: Emotions

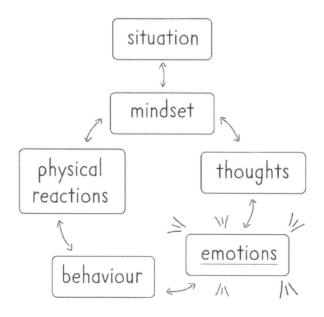

PART FOUR: EMOTIONS
4.1: Three Key Points About the Psychology of Emotions

"Happiness is not something ready-made. It comes from your own actions." – Dalai Lama.

In the last two years, Polly's new mindsets, thoughts, and behaviours have reduced her negative emotions and enhanced her positive emotions. When we experience a lot of stress and anxiety, *all* our negative emotions intensify. We might feel:

- A sense of dread,
- Afraid,
- Low mood,
- Irritable,
- Impatient,
- Tense,
- Anger,
- Guilt,
- Paranoia.

Transforming and reducing our stress, autostress and anxiety is therefore incredibly powerful, as it has the potential to help us reduce a wide range of negative emotions. As we're covering how to tackle negative emotions in the rest of The Framework, in this section, we'll be focusing on happiness.

Key Point 1: Positive and Negative Wellbeing States Can Occur at The Same Time
In her TED Talk, psychologist Nancy Etcoff from Harvard Medical School describes our two parallel systems of mental health: mental unwellness and mental wellness.

You see, mental health isn't a single continuum, as it seems to feel intuitively. To become less miserable doesn't necessarily mean we become happier. The absence of mental unwellness is not mental wellness.

mental unwellness   mental wellness

Our two parallel systems of mental health would've allowed our ancient ancestors to look for opportunity at the same time as avoiding danger. This explains why it's possible to suffer from stress, autostress and anxiety but at the same time feel happy.

Negative thinking habits come easier to us than positive thinking habits because we have an ingrained and powerful negativity bias. As avoiding danger was extremely important for our ancient ancestors, negative emotions have a stronger impact on us than positive emotions, we process negative information more easily and quickly, and we react more intensely to negative stimuli than to equally strong positive stimuli. The struggle is real—for a lot of us, it takes real effort to be happy!

Happiness is a skill, so, how do we do it?

Key Point 2: Emotions Are Best Seen as a By-Product
As the opening quote from the Dalai Lama stated, happiness comes from our own actions. It's best understood as a *by-product* of what we do–the mindsets we adopt, the thoughts we focus on, and our behaviour.

When it comes to the type of thoughts that give rise to happiness, the BOP method is a perfect example of what we should be focusing on: thoughts that are balanced, optimistic and proactive.

When it comes to happiness-inducing behaviours, researcher Lahnna Catalino explains, "people who pursue happiness by seeking out pleasant experiences as part of their everyday lives are happier." It's all about discovering our nourishing activities, knowing what brings us joy, and making it happen! There are lots of free mood tracking apps available that can help us become more aware of what makes us most happy. You might be surprised by what you discover!

Catalino also warns us: "In stark contrast, people who strive to feel good every possible moment, as if it were possible to will oneself to be happy, appear to be following a recipe for unhappiness." This is why it's so important to focus on happiness as a *by-product*, not seeing it as something we can make happen just like that.

It's also important to note that sometimes we have no control over our mood regardless of the mindsets, thoughts and behaviours we adopt. Our mood naturally fluctuates. For women, changes in hormones during the second half of the menstrual cycle can lead to mood swings, anxiety and irritability, which ease and disappear when the period starts (second half, as in, for a full two weeks!). Each woman's experience of this is different and might vary from month to month. However, nearly *all* women experience some kind of premenstrual symptom. So, it's important to enjoy the positive moods whilst they're there, and know that bad moods will pass, and are often outside of our control. When you notice what feels like a random bad mood, you might find the following mantra useful: *'this too shall pass'.*

Key Point 3: Using the Two Arrows of Happiness Mindset

When it comes to mindsets for happiness, by far the most powerful is what I call The Two Arrows of Happiness mindset. This mindset is inspired by the popular Buddhist metaphor, The Two Arrows of Suffering. Buddhists say that any time we experience misfortune, two arrows come our way. The first arrow is the actual bad event, which can, indeed, cause real pain. The second arrow is the suffering, which represents our response to the bad event. This short quote from Buddha sums it up: *"pain is inevitable, suffering is optional."*

So, what does this have to do with the Two Arrows of Happiness? Well, it's the same principle. Anytime we experience fortune, we have the first arrow: the joy we experience in that moment. To boost our happiness levels, we can intentionally fire the first arrow more often, making an effort to plan more pleasant experiences into our lives.

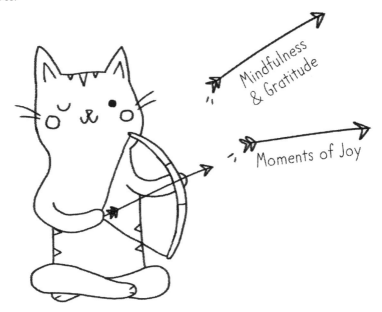

Second, we can choose to fire the second arrow of happiness which is prolonging and intensifying our experience of joy. We can do this by adopting an attitude of gratitude and practising mindfulness during our experience of happiness and pleasure. It's all about making an effort to be fully present when it's happening and appreciating it during and after it happens.

The more we shoot The Two Arrows of Happiness, the happier we become. This is what makes gratitude journaling one of the most effective interventions in the field of positive psychology (the study of happiness). Research shows that people who practise gratitude are more likely to be happier and more optimistic, which studies suggest boosts our immune system.

Polly used to think that her temperament meant her mood would always be pretty neutral. She never really felt an ongoing positive mood, which made her dislike the word 'happy'. She thought of happiness as a bit of a myth. However, since practising the skills we describe in The Framework, she regularly experiences a stable positive mood and now considers herself a happy person!

We can think of positive and negative moods as being like a pair of scales with positive and negative mood *states* as the weighing substance. The more positive experiences we have, the more positive our overall mood will be.

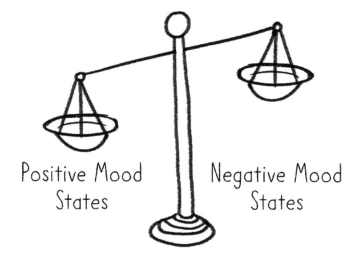

Positive Mood States

Negative Mood States

In other words, happiness is a state of mind that becomes a state of brain. Dr Rick Hanson, an expert in the neuroscience of happiness, explains:

> *"By taking just a few extra seconds to stay with a positive experience—even the comfort in a single breath—you'll help turn a passing mental state into lasting neural structure."*

We'll explain more about what this means in the final part of The Framework!

SUMMARY 4.1
Our emotions are best viewed as by-products. Changing them is achieved by optimising our mindsets, thoughts and behaviour.

To experience less negative emotions, we can focus on the methods described for reducing stress, autostress and anxiety outlined throughout The Framework.

To experience more positive emotions, we can use the BOP method and adopt the Two Arrows of Happiness Mindset, making an effort to have more positive experiences, and focusing our thoughts on being grateful and present.

In the next section, we'll discover the most effective behaviours for helping ourselves feel calmer and happier.

PART FIVE: Behaviour

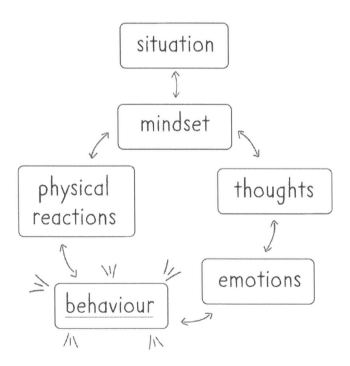

PART FIVE: BEHAVIOUR
5.1: Overcoming Avoidance and Safety Behaviours

"A ship in harbour is safe, but that is not what ships are built for." – John A. Shedd.

When Polly moved to her new city she wanted to meet new people but at the same time she felt her stress response and anxiety held her back. She wanted to avoid the discomfort she felt in these situations. This meant she'd turn down invitations to social outings, and at work, she kept herself to herself and didn't make much of an effort to socialise.

Though avoiding discomfort gives us temporary relief, it prevents us from realising we're stronger, more capable, and more resilient than we think. When we avoid things, we limit our ability to live life to the full. Chloe Brotheridge, author of The Anxiety Solution, explains how people with anxiety often have difficulties 'leaning in'. She explains:

> *"One thing I've learnt about women who have anxiety is that we have a problem 'leaning in' to things in general, whether it's speaking up, taking risks, or putting ourselves out there. Leaning in can feel risky and unsafe. It means we're stepping into the unknown; we don't trust ourselves, and, yup, we're afraid of losing control. But leaning into life, taking on challenges, pushing ourselves a little out of our comfort zones, and taking a few risks is essential if we're to overcome anxiety."*

When we lean into life, we lean into uncertainty. People who experience anxiety have been shown to have a low tolerance for uncertainty. It's worth reminding ourselves that uncertainty is an inescapable part of life, and the sooner we become comfortable with it, the sooner we can reduce stress and anxiety. As John Allen Paulos notes: *"uncertainty is the only certainty there is, and knowing how to live with insecurity is the only security."*

To deal with uncertainty, we often resort to what psychologists call 'safety behaviours'. Safety behaviours are the things we do to feel safer, but they can end up making us feel worse in the long run. Like avoidance, they prevent us from realising we're stronger, more capable, and more resilient than we think.

An example of a common safety behaviour is relying on alcohol in social situations. For example, Polly used to make sure she had a couple of drinks before any social event she went to. She decided she wanted to feel more comfortable around new people and not rely on alcohol, so she started to gradually build up her social interactions. Here's what she did:

1) First, she started making more conversation with people at work. She stopped going out by herself for lunch and brought in packed lunch and ate it in the kitchen. She introduced herself to people and asked how their week was going

2) She decided to build on her confidence by downloading Bumble BFF, an app for meeting new people. Whilst her initial discomfort was high, her stress response and anxiety reduced over time with the more people she met

3) Next, she started accepting invitations to more social outings, and didn't go home early like she used to. She stopped having drinks beforehand, and instead focused on telling herself to 'get excited', looking forward to opportunity to meet new people, and reminding herself that the more she goes to these events, the more comfortable she'll feel. She also allowed herself to feel a sense of achievement after each event she went to

SUMMARY 5.1
The longer we use avoidance and safety behaviours as coping mechanisms, the more our brain believes the activities we're avoiding are threats. This ends up causing us more stress, autostress and anxiety in the long run, and blocks us from experiencing personal growth.

To feel our best selves, we need to cultivate our habit of leaning into uncertainty and challenging ourselves to step outside of our comfort zone.

5.2: Calming Autostress by Practising Relaxation

"We humans have lost the wisdom of genuinely resting and relaxing. We worry too much. We don't allow our bodies to heal, and we don't allow our minds and hearts to heal." – Thich Nhat Hanh.

By the time Polly was at university, she was experiencing her stress response symptoms on an ongoing basis; she'd entered a state of autostress. Some of Polly's personal autostress symptoms include:

- Breathing difficulties,
- Excessive yawning,
- Chest tightness,
- Heart pounding and racing,
- Heart palpitations,
- Irregular heartbeat,
- Muscle tension,
- Ringing in the ear.

When she wasn't aware all her symptoms were related to autostress, she spent a lot of time on Google trying to figure out what might be wrong with her, and often came to some scary conclusions! Once, she rang an ambulance because she was worried she had a scary heart condition. She ended up having an electrocardiogram (ECG) at the hospital, a test that checks your heart's rhythm and electrical activity. When everything came back normal, she felt relieved, but also confused and worried about what was wrong.

Now she understands her symptoms are related to autostress, she feels like a weight has been lifted from her shoulders because she understands how to deal with it. To reduce autostress, we need to increase activity of our parasympathetic nervous system. We'll be exploring the science behind this further in the final section of The Framework.

Her favourite way of activating her parasympathetic nervous system is through practising relaxation. She was so used to being on the go 24/7, she found it difficult to relax at first. She realised she was putting too much pressure on herself to be productive all the time, but eventually, she started seeing relaxation practises as form of productivity, too.

It took her a few months to get into it, but the more she practised, the calmer she felt. Her favourite relaxation practise is deep breathing. When we're autostressed, we often develop breathing difficulties. We can even be holding our breath without realising it.

Breathing difficulties are actually the root cause of the most common physical symptoms associated with stress.

When we have breathing difficulties, we lower the amount of carbon dioxide that's normally in our blood. This leads to a wide range of symptoms associated with stress including:

- Shortness of breath,
- Chest tightness,
- Tingling or numbness in the arms, fingers, toes, or around the mouth,
- Feeling dizzy and light-headed,
- Weakness,
- Heart pounding and racing,
- Heart palpitations,
- Sweating or hot flushes,
- Headaches,
- Feeling sick,
- Fatigue.

These symptoms can all appear out of the blue. If you ever feel anxious and have no idea why, this might explain things. We might be:

1) *Shallow breathing* (breathing in too quickly),
2) *Over-breathing* (breathing in more air as we feel like we're not getting enough, for example through yawning or sighing frequently).

Some people experience both.

So, let's take a moment to test our breathing:

- Put one hand on your chest, and one on your belly.
- Breathe for a few seconds. Which hand rises?
- If it's your chest, you might have developed a habit of shallow breathing.

Although the effects of shallow breathing can be very unpleasant, it won't harm you, and we can reverse the habit by practising deeper breathing. The next time you feel stressed, take a moment to notice your breathing. Focus on breathing through your stomach, so that your belly rises when you inhale and drops when you exhale. Here's a deep breathing exercise we can practise for 5 minutes a day to help us feel calmer:

- Inhale deeply and slowly count to four, expanding your belly as you do so,
- Hold that breath for a count of two,
- Slowly exhale though your mouth for a count of six.

This is what we call '4-2-6 belly breathing'. Research shows that practicing this regularly can significantly reduce stress symptoms within a matter of weeks.

breathe in
through the
belly

SUMMARY 5.2

To reduce autostress, we need to increase activity of our parasympathetic nervous system. One way to do this is through practicing relaxation. Some ways we can practise relaxation including the following:

- 4-2-6 belly breathing,
- Progressive muscle relaxation,
- Visualisation,
- Yoga,
- Pilates,
- Tai Chi,
- Massages,
- Gentle stretching,

- Spending time in nature,
- Mindful colouring,
- Listening to music,
- Warm baths,
- Playing a musical instrument,
- A creative activity (such as drawing and painting),
- Floatation therapy,
- Doing a digital detox.

Remember, mental wellness is complex—different things work at different times for different people. For some people, things will be relaxing, for others, not so much. Try and test and discover what works best for you!

bonus cat

I highly recommend the apps Pacifica and Calm for practicing relaxation. Pacifica has a wide range of features for enhancing mental wellness, including a free 9 minute progressive muscle relaxation exercise. The Calm app focuses on meditation but also includes a free breathing tool.

5.3: Meeting Our Basic Needs: Rest and Sleep

"The current male-dominated model of success—which equates success with burnout, sleep deprivation, and driving yourself into the ground—isn't working for women, and it's not working for men, either." – Arianna Huffington

In 3.1, we heard that when we miss out on our basic needs, we can experience the stress response. For the remainder of this section we'll look more into why meeting those basic needs; rest, exercise, social connection and nutrition, is so vital for our mental wellness.

We live in a society that glorifies being busy. So much so that presenteeism— attending work despite being unwell—actually costs the economy more than general absenteeism. When we ignore our body, forgo basic needs and overwork ourselves, we increase our risk of exhaustion and burnout. This will ultimately lead to larger periods off work, so it's vital we listen to our body.

Fortunately, there are many managers that understand the importance of looking after our mental health. Take Ben Congleton for example. Here's what he had to say when his employee, Madalyn, explained to her colleagues that she was taking a mental health day:

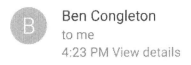

Hey Madalyn,

I just wanted to personally thank you for sending emails like this. Every time you do, I use it as a reminder of the importance of using sick days for mental health -- I can't believe this is not standard practice at all organizations. You are an example to us all, and help cut through the stigma so we can all bring our whole selves to work.

Now, let's take a deeper look into the importance of sleep.

Sleep deprivation is both a cause and a consequence of stress, autostress and anxiety. Studies show that a lack of sleep can lead to a more active amygdala—the part of the brain that generates stress. When we're sleep deprived, getting less than 7 hours sleep a night, there will likely be an increase in cortisol and adrenaline in our system.

As the NHS website explains:

"When people with anxiety or depression were surveyed to calculate their sleeping habits, it turned out that most of them slept for less than six hours a night. One in three of us suffers from poor sleep, with stress, computers and taking work home often blamed. However, the cost of all those sleepless nights is more than just bad moods and a lack of focus. Regular poor sleep puts you at risk of serious medical conditions, including obesity, heart disease and diabetes—and it shortens your life expectancy. It's now clear that a solid night's sleep is essential for a long and healthy life."

It's therefore very important to develop good habits that give ourselves the best chance of getting a decent night's sleep. Here are four key areas to consider:

1) Addressing Our Anxiety

Often what keeps us most awake is actually our anxiety, especially if we don't have much time to think during the day. Practising cognitive defusion and cognitive restructuring techniques, as I've described, can be very helpful for bedtime anxiety. Making a note of worries and reviewing them at the end of the day can also be very helpful for reducing bedtime anxiety—especially for the common experience of Sunday night anxiety.

Negative thoughts about sleep itself are particularly disruptive—when our thoughts are along the lines of 'I'm going to get an awful night's sleep and feel so tired tomorrow', we're setting ourselves up for more anxiety and a self-fulfilling prophecy.

In a podcast interview with Dr Ranjan Chatterjee*, co-founder of The Sleep School Dr Guy Meadows says that in his experience, telling people about the physiology of sleep can be a powerful way to reduce anxiety. The key information he tells patients is this: we sleep in cycles of 1.5-2 hours long. At the end of each cycle, we've evolved to come up and check for danger—our poor ancestors probably wouldn't have survived an 8 hour sleep! This means that during the short gaps between cycles, we can become briefly alert. Waking up in the night is a natural physiological process. It's a myth that we should be able to sleep for 8 hours non-stop! Worrying during these natural waking periods is a key driver of sleep deprivation.

So, what can we do? Instead of becoming frustrated and worrying about not getting enough sleep, we could use cognitive restructuring with the following kinds of thoughts:

"I've woken up in the middle of the night—this is annoying, but natural. I might sleep more, or I might not. It's not a total disaster if I don't. I'll get up and do something then come back to bed if I don't fall back to sleep soon."

---

* The podcast is called Feel Better, Live More and the episode is 'Good Sleep Habits and Sleep Misconceptions'—highly recommended!

"It took me ages to swtich off earlier and after finally getting to sleep, I've woken up again. I must be at the end of a sleep cycle. At least I've got a bit of sleep. I'll try focusing my attention on my breathing again and hopefully I'll get back to sleep. I can only do my best."

"If I don't get a good night's sleep that's OK, I'll get an early night tomorrow."

When we're having trouble dozing off, one of the worst things we can do is to keep checking our phones. First, the bright light wakes our brains up more. Second, checking the time can end up causing more anxiety.

2) Creating A Bedtime Routine
Creating a bedtime routine can send a signal to our brain that it'll eventually associate with sleep. Once the association is made, our brains will start producing melatonin, our sleep hormone.

Our night time ritual could include writing in a journal (which, as I've mentioned, can be especially helpful for reducing anxiety). We could practise deep breathing, meditation, lighting a candle, reading a book, or listening to relaxing music (why not make a bedtime playlist?).

Many people find it helpful to set an alarm thirty minutes to one hour before bed time to alert us it's time to start winding down.

It's best to avoid things other than sleep and sex in bed. Our brains are more primed to think about work if we get into the habit of checking emails and using our laptop in bed, which can lead to more anxiety.

One last thing—tablet and mobile phone screens are best avoided for at least an hour up until bed time. The artificial light interferes with our brain's sleep hormones, so much so that just 20 minutes of looking at our phone has the same effect on our brains as a 2 hour walk in daylight! You might want to actually charge your phone in a different room to where you sleep, that way you remove the temptation all together. You can use an 'old fashioned' alarm clock to replace your phone or tablet!

3) Optimising Our Diet
Here's what to avoid consuming when it comes to boosting our chances of getting a good night's rest:

- **Caffeinated drinks**—avoiding coffee, tea (including green tea) and many Coca-Cola drinks after 2-3pm helps our body wind down before bedtime

- **Alcohol**—whilst many people believe that having a night-cap will help them sleep, it's been shown to lead to interrupted sleep and early waking
- **Sugar and simple carbs**—these can cause a rise in blood sugar which makes us feel more alert
- **Protein snacks**—protein can also make us feel more alert; it blocks the synthesis of serotonin, which helps promote sleep

4) Optimising Our Environment

Because a slight dip in body temperature promotes good sleep, your bedroom should be cooler compared to your other rooms in your home, but not too cold! This also makes our nightwear choice important—we should avoid wearing pyjamas or bedtime socks that'll make us too hot, as it risks waking us up.

Here are final 3 tips regarding our environment from Nick Littlehales, sports sleep coach and author of the book Sleep:

1. Invest in a super king size mattress if you sleep with another person and have the space. If you don't, it's worth trying to create space, for example, by moving your bedside table
2. Try a dawn-wake simulator which recreates the sunrise in your bedroom to help you wake naturally and make it easier to get out of bed. Reputable brands include Lumie and Philips
3. Buy hypoallergenic bedding even if you don't suffer from allergies and make sure it's breathable to help keep you cool

SUMMARY 5.3

Getting enough rest and sleep is crucial to our mental health. Research shows that people who are sleep deprived are more likely to experience stress and anxiety, possibly because it leads to our amygdala being more active and higher levels of stress hormones in our system.

Like the stress-anxiety loop, we can experience a mental unwellness-sleep deprivation loop. The worse our mental health, the worse our sleep; the worse our sleep, the worse our mental health.

There are plenty of changes we can make to improve our sleeping habits, the most important being addressing our anxiety.

There's one important habit for improving sleep we haven't yet mentioned: exercise. We'll explore the wide-ranging benefits of exercise in the next section.

5.4: Meeting Our Basic Needs: Exercise

"Walking is man's best medicine." – Hippocrates.

Exercise has an extremely wide range of health benefits. We tend to think of exercise as a healthy habit, but in fact, I'd argue it's a basic need. Our bodies are designed to expend a great amount of energy, and when they don't, it negatively impacts our minds and bodies. Lack of exercise is associated with both mental health difficulties and chronic illness.

So, what happens to us when we exercise that makes it so important for our mental and physical health? Here's 10 key benefits:

1. **Improved Sleep**
Research shows that people who exercise regularly fall asleep faster, sleep longer, have better quality sleep and wake up less often during the night. One study suggests the improvement in sleep quality after 150 minutes of moderate to vigorous exercise per week is 65%. Yep, 65% better quality sleep! Exercising in the late afternoon and early evening is best, as it promotes a dip in our night time body temperature which helps us sleep. On the other hand, exercising less than 3 hours before bed can have the opposite effect, increasing our body temperature and interfering with a good night's sleep.

2. **Reduced Stress Response**
Exercise reduces the overall activation of our amygdala and sympathetic nervous system—the parts of our brain and body that generate the stress response. It burns excess adrenaline and blood sugar, which helps us feel calmer and reduces our blood pressure. Exercise also provides us with a distraction from negative thoughts and worries, reducing anxiety.

3. **Reduced Muscle Tension**
Exercise helps relax our muscles, which can make us feel more relaxed for up to hours afterwards.

4. **Confidence Boost**
There's so many elements about exercise that helps boost our confidence: a feeling of achievement after each workout, our body's toning up, weight loss, a positive change in our skin and developing the ability to go outside of our comfort zone, to name just a few! This new-found confidence all helps boost our mood.

5. **Boosts Endorphins and Serotonin**
Another way exercise helps boost our mood is through the release of endorphins and

serotonin, our brain's feel-good chemicals. Endorphins help us feel happier and calmer and are a naturally pain reliever.

One study showed that people who completed an aerobic exercise class had higher levels of serotonin and improved mood compared to a group who completed a stretching class.

6. **Protection from Injuries and Aches**
Exercise makes our muscles stronger and more flexible, supporting our bones and joints and making it less likely that we pull a muscle or suffer from injuries and aches.

7. **Protection from Chronic Illness**
Lack of exercise increases our risk of coronary heart disease, diabetes, hypertension, Alzheimer's, and some cancers.

8. **Improves Digestion**
Working out can help us absorb vital vitamins and minerals which help us feel calm. (We'll explore more about the importance of this in section 5.6!)

9. **Increased Oxygenation of Our Blood and Brain**
Exercise increases our alertness and ability to focus by increasing blood flow to the brain.

10. **Increased Neurogenesis**
Exercise stimulates chemicals in the brain called "brain derived neurotrophic factors" which help new brain cells to grow and develop. New research suggests that anti-depressants exert their effects by stimulating neurogenesis. The process of neurogenesis results in a stronger foundation for us to learn new knowledge and skills, such as mental wellness skills!

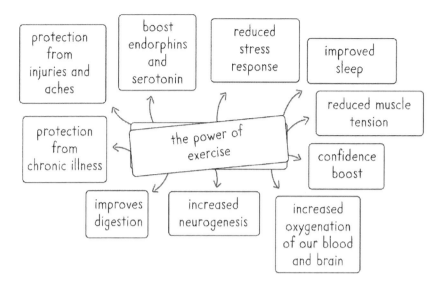

With such wide-ranging benefits and no negative side effects, it's no wonder doctors regularly prescribe exercise as a mental health intervention! It's a shame doctors don't have the time to properly explain all the benefits so that their patients understood just how powerful it is.

A study by Professor Steven Petruzzello showed that just 10 weeks of regular exercise was enough to reduce people's general level of anxiety.

Research suggests that aerobic exercise (such as walking, cycling, and jogging) provides the same benefits as non-aerobic exercise (such as yoga and pilates). Studies also suggest we need around 21 minutes three times a week to experience the benefits. So, we don't have to spend hours doing it—it's something most of us can fit in to our lives when it becomes a priority. It could be something as simple as committing to get off public transport a stop earlier and power walking to and from work.

It's important to find something that suits us and that we enjoy—exercising doesn't have to mean the gym, if that's not your thing. Now more people than ever are interested in fitness, we have a large variety of classes and sports available to try. If you have the room, YouTube and 'bedroom fitness' is another popular option to try.

And remember, it's very common to not feel like exercising. We can't rely on motivation to exercise; motivation is an emotion, so, it naturally fluctuates. Motivation comes with action. Once we begin exercising, that's when we get into it.

SUMMARY 5.4
Our bodies are designed for exercise. There's been a lot of research conducted into the effects of exercise on mental health which repeatedly suggests it can significantly

reduce the symptoms of stress, autostress and anxiety. Research even suggests that it can enhance our mental wellness just as much as psychotherapy.

Buddying up with someone can make it easier to develop our exercise habit. Exercise buddies give us the powerful combination of support, accountability, and even healthy competition.

In the next section, we'll explore why having an exercise buddy taps into another of our basic needs: social connection.

5.5: Meeting Our Basic Needs: Social Connection

"Of all the means which are procured by wisdom to ensure happiness throughout the whole of life, by far the most important is the acquisition of friends." – Epicurus.

In ancestral times, being part of a community was vital to our survival. There's now considerable evidence that suggests that, on the whole, compared with people in previous decades, we spend less time with family and friends. We have fewer close friends and are less involved in our communities. This affects our physical health as well as our mental health; research shows that the health risk of social isolation is comparable to the risks of smoking, high blood pressure and lack of exercise.

It's not surprising then, that The Mental Health Foundation calls relationships "the forgotten foundation of mental health and wellbeing". They explain:

> *"People who are more socially connected to family, friends, or their community are happier, physically healthier and live longer, with fewer mental health problems than people who are less well connected. It's not just the number of friends you have, and it's not whether or not you're in a committed relationship, but it's the quality of your close relationships that matters."*

In fact, the longest-running study on happiness found that the quality of our social connections is the single biggest predictor of happiness. Our relationships have more power over our happiness than genes, IQ, social class, money, or fame. The director of the study, Robert Waldinger, notes "the surprising finding is that our relationships and how happy we are in our relationships has a powerful influence on our health."

When it comes to priorities for mental wellness, our relationships deserve a top spot. The new science of stress even suggests we release a hormone, oxytocin, that encourages us to seek social support during stressful times. Research suggests that women release more oxytocin. This has been called the 'tend and befriend' response to stress. 'Tending' refers to caring for ourselves and our children, whereas 'befriending' refers to seeking social support.

Relating to this is a theory about women's higher life expectancies; the hypothesis is that the male response to stress (which includes higher levels of social withdrawal, aggression, and substance abuse) puts them at higher risk for adverse health-related consequences. In contrast, the 'tend and befriend' response used more by women has been shown to reduce our stress response by lowering heart rate, blood pressure, and cortisol, and thus is protective to health.

Polly considers herself an introvert, and she used to think that she didn't need much social support or interaction. However, her beliefs on this have changed since she's become happier—she's found that she wants to socialise more, and doing so reliably boosts her mood. It feels like a positive feedback loop.

Studies in fact back this up: it's been found that compared with people experiencing a neutral mood, people experiencing positive mood show greater sociability, sense of connection, self-disclosure, trust in others, and compassion. Plus, the more time people devote to generating positive emotions in themselves, the more pleasant their interactions with others become.

Psychologist Barbara Fredrickson, a leading researcher in the field of positive emotions, labels this the 'upward spiral' of positive emotions and health. Her research suggests social connection is a key factor in happiness and is associated with changes in our vagus nerve, an important component of the parasympathetic nervous system.

Fredrickson carried out a study exploring this with Bethany Kok and colleagues in 2013. Half of the study participants attended a 6-week loving-kindness meditation (LKM) course, which involved learning how to cultivate positive feelings of love, compassion and goodwill toward ourselves and others. They were asked to practice meditation at home, but how often they meditated was up to them. The other half of the participants remained on a waiting list for the course.

For 61 consecutive days, participants in both groups reported their meditation, prayer, or solo spiritual activity, their emotional experiences and their social interactions within the last day. Their vagal tone—the activity of their vagus nerve—was assessed twice, once at the beginning and once at the end of the study.

The findings suggested that positive emotions, positive social connections, and vagal tone does indeed give rise to an upward-spiral dynamic. They found that greater positive emotions prompted people to see themselves as more socially connected. Over time, as moments of positive emotions and positive social connections increased, vagal tone also improved.

Fredrickson explains:

> *"The daily moments of connection that people feel with others emerge as the tiny engines that drive the upward spiral between positivity and health."*

SUMMARY 5.5
Social connection is well established as one of our core basic needs that help make us the happiest, healthiest versions of ourselves.

There's lots of great books and guidance online for how to improve our relationships.

There's also now plenty of ways to meet new people with the help of technology. Check out the apps Meetup, Bumble BFF, Hey! VINA, MeetMe, and Skout.

In the final section on behaviour, we'll explore the impact of meeting our basic need of nourishing nutrition.

5.6: Meeting Our Basic Needs: Nutrition

"Let food be thy medicine, and medicine be thy food." – Hippocrates.

Our diet and mood are interconnected; what we eat has the power to make us feel better or worse. We need nourishing foods to fulfil our brain's essential neurochemistry.

When we eat, the food is absorbed into our GI tract, a.k.a., our gut. Vitamins, minerals and amino acids are carried through our bloodstream and into our brain. Enzymes then convert our amino acids into neurotransmitters, such as serotonin, dopamine and GABA. These neurotransmitters are chemicals that help us keep calm, sleep well, increase our feelings of pleasure, and more!

Signs that our diet isn't nourishing enough include:

- Anxiety and low mood,
- Mood swings and irritability,
- Low energy,
- Stomach pain,
- Gas,
- Bloating,
- Diarrhoea,
- Heartburn,
- Indigestion,
- Poor memory and concentration.

Here are some top food and drink tips to ensure your diet is helping you feel your best self.

Top Food Tips

1. Make Your Meals Balanced, Regular and Easily Digestible

Balanced meals consist of around half vegetables, quarter complex carbohydrates (such as whole grains) and quarter protein. An example of a balanced meal would be broccoli, brown rice and fish. Chloe McLeod, a dietician, says *"for most people whose plates look like that, it's going to mean better health because you're filling up on more of the lower energy foods and getting more of those micronutrients [vitamins and minerals] found more so in the vegetables"*.

We should try to avoid high levels of trans fat. We can spot them by looking for 'hydrogenated' or 'partially hydrogenated' on food ingredients lists. The Food and Drug Administration removed the 'generally recognized as safe' label from trans fats, following studies that strongly linked them with cardiovascular problems such as heart disease. The best way to avoid them is by eliminating the amount of processed food in our diet. Cooking from scratch is key!

Healthy fats, on the other hand, are very important for mental health. Balance here is also key. Most people eat too many Omega-6 fatty acids and not enough Omega-3 fatty acids. It's thought this distorted ratio might actually be one of the most damaging aspects of the Western diet. By far the best and healthiest way to increase your Omega-3 intake is to eat seafood once or twice per week. Fatty fish like salmon is a particularly good source. If you don't eat seafood, you could consider taking a fish oil supplement (cod liver oil is best, because it's high in Vitamin D and Vitamin A).

Experts suggest that eating five small meals or three smaller meals with two snacks is better than eating three large meals a day. This is because large meals can be taxing for our digestive system and affect our mood and energy levels. When we eat a big meal, our blood sugar level rises. Once the meal is digested, our blood sugar level falls, causing our mood and energy to fall with it. The bigger the meal, the bigger the crash.

2.   Manage Your Blood Sugar

This brings us onto the important point of managing our blood sugar. We all know that sugar is super tasty, and it can be highly addictive, too. When we eat sugar our brain releases dopamine, the same neurotransmitter that's released when people have cocaine.

Having too much sugar leads not only to unstable moods and energy crashes, but can also lead to what's called reactive hypoglycaemia. Reactive hypoglycaemia is low blood sugar that occurs 1 to 3 hours after you eat food high in sugar. Symptoms are very similar to anxiety—you might sweat and feel shaky or weak or develop a headache. Some people are more reactive to sugar than others. If you experience these symptoms, you should eat a healthy meal as soon as possible.

In the long-term, too much sugar is also associated with premature brain ageing and reduced neuroplasticity. We need neuroplasticity—the ability of our brain to rewire itself—to become our calmer and happier selves.

3.   Help Your Good Bacteria Flourish

It turns out we're just as much bacteria as we are human. The latest research suggests we have the same number of bacteria cells as we have human cells. Keeping our gut bacteria healthy is essential for a healthy mind and body. It's believed our gut's microbiotic environment influences the functioning of our amygdala and prefrontal cortex—the key areas of our brain involved in stress and anxiety. This is why our gut is now often referred to as our 'second brain'. To help your good bacteria flourish, you could try adding into your diet:

- Probiotic and prebiotic capsules.
- Fermented foods like yoghurt, kimchi, and sauerkraut.
- Pulses, legumes, garlic, onion, apples, chickpeas, leeks, dates, figs, and asparagus, which are all thought to help good bacteria flourish.

Top Drink Tips

1. Stay Hydrated
Our bodies are around 80% water. Each day we lose around 4% of our water weight through sweating, urinating and even breathing. If we don't replace our natural water loss, we can experience symptoms of dehydration which mimic those of the stress response—dizziness, light-headedness and a faster heartbeat. In climates such as the UK's, we should aim for around six to eight glasses of water a day to stop us getting dehydrated.

2. Limit Caffeine
Caffeine is found in coffee, tea (including green tea), chocolate, cola, and energy drinks. Like sugar, we all vary in how sensitive we are to caffeine. In most people, it can increase mental alertness and concentration, but too much can leave us experiencing nervousness, insomnia, and heart palpitations.

This is because caffeine activates our body's stress response—it can increase our blood pressure and raise stress hormones such as cortisol. It can also deplete B vitamins, especially thiamin, which is needed for producing GABA, a neurotransmitter that helps keeps us calm. This can lead to the vicious cycle shown on the following page.

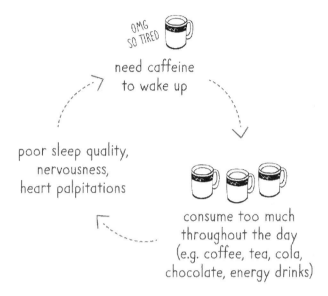

the vicious cycle of caffeine overuse

OMG
SO TIRED

need caffeine
to wake up

poor sleep quality,
nervousness,
heart palpitations

consume too much
throughout the day
(e.g. coffee, tea, cola,
chocolate, energy drinks)

As I mentioned in section 5.3, as caffeine can cause insomnia and poor sleep quality, it's best avoided after 2-3pm.

3.   Limit Alcohol

I also mentioned in section 5.3 that alcohol can have adverse effects on our mental health. Whilst many people believe that having a drink will help them sleep, it's been shown to lead to interrupted sleep and early waking. Many people also use alcohol to help feel calmer. Although it can calm us down initially, it actually increases our anxiety in the long run because it lowers our levels of GABA, the calming neurotransmitter.

A study by registered nutritional therapist Amanda Geary in 1998 surveyed 165 people who were using nutrition specifically to improve their mental health. She found that over one third of people felt that improving their diet had directly improved their mental health.

When it came to cutting down or avoiding potential food 'stressors', the top 3 strategies found to be most helpful were:

1.   Cutting down on sugar (80% of people found useful),
2.   Cutting down on caffeine (79% of people found useful),

3. Cutting down on alcohol (55% of people found useful).

SUMMARY 5.6
Meeting our basic need of a nourishing diet is an important part of becoming our calmer and happier selves. A nourishing diet involves balanced, regular, easily digestible meals, stable blood sugar, and a decent dose of healthy bacteria. It's also important to stay hydrated and limit our caffeine and alcohol intake if we're seriously committed to optimal mental wellness.

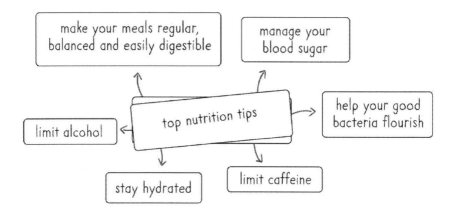

Next, we're onto the final section of The Framework: physical reactions.

overactive
amygdala
club

PART SIX: Physical Reactions

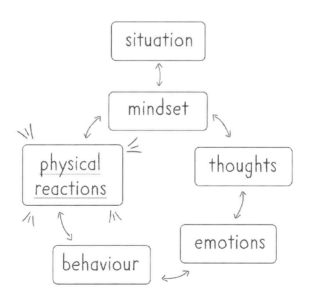

PART SIX: PHYSICAL REACTIONS
6.1: Calming the Amygdala

"Your body hears everything your mind says." – Naomi Judd.

By now, we hope you'll have realised our minds and bodies are extremely interconnected!

We've already heard about common physical reactions to stress, autostress and anxiety throughout The Framework. This section is about putting what we've learnt all together: understanding more about the science behind what's happening in our brain and bodies when we become calmer and happier. Hugely complex neurological and physiological processes are involved. We won't go into massive technical detail, but will instead provide simplified explanations that help you understand more about the mechanisms behind the methods I've described.

Here's a reminder of the common unpleasant physical reactions associated with stress:

- Heart pounding and racing,
- Heart palpitations,
- Irregular heartbeat,
- Feeling dizzy and light-headed,
- Neck and shoulder tension,
- Clenched jaw,
- Grinding your teeth (especially at night),
- Headaches,
- General aches, pains and tense muscles,
- Shaking hands and legs,
- Breathing difficulties (for example, feeling as though you can't get enough air),
- Excessive yawning,
- Faster breathing,
- Chest tightness,
- Sweating or hot flushes,
- Pins and needles,
- IBS,
- Restlessness,
- Low energy,
- Ringing in the ear,
- Tingling or numbness in the arms, fingers, toes, or around the mouth,

- Feeling sick,
- Fatigue,
- Frequent urination,
- Changes in sex drive,
- Frequent colds,
- Feelings of unreality (of the self and the world).

It's very important to be aware of our physical reactions and what triggers them. This takes practise. We often don't notice our physical reactions straight away because we're focusing on what's causing our distress, not on how it impacts us physically. When we become more mindful of what's happening in our body, we can take quicker and more effective action to help ourselves feel better. It's like the old saying goes, *"if you listen to your body when it whispers, you won't have to hear it scream."*

Next time you feel stressed, try tuning into your body. Scan the length of your body, noticing what it feels like. See if there's any clenching, tightness or aching. Common areas people hold stress in their bodies include the jaw, neck and shoulders. We can then make an effort to relax them if we notice they're tense.

We can also notice if our breath has shortened or quickened and do some deep breathing to help us feel more relaxed. A great way to enhance self-awareness of our physical sensations is to practise a body scan meditation, which you can do using meditation apps such as Calm and Headspace.

Noticing our stress response can also give us a better insight into our thoughts and emotions. We may realise we're in a cycle of hypothetical worry or rumination, and we can then take steps to escape our downward spiralling with cognitive defusion or cognitive restructuring techniques.

All of this helps us calm the amygdala, the part of our brain that generates the stress response. In people who experience a lot of stress, autostress and anxiety, their amygdala is overactive. Therefore, when we use the techniques described in The Framework and become calmer, our amygdala becomes calmer, too.

Our amygdala triggers our body's stress response by signalling a part of our brain called the hypothalamus to release a substance called CRF. CRF then alerts our pituitary gland to release another substance called ACTH into our bloodstream. ACTH triggers our adrenal glands, located at the top of our kidneys, to release adrenaline and noradrenaline, which activates our sympathetic nervous system.

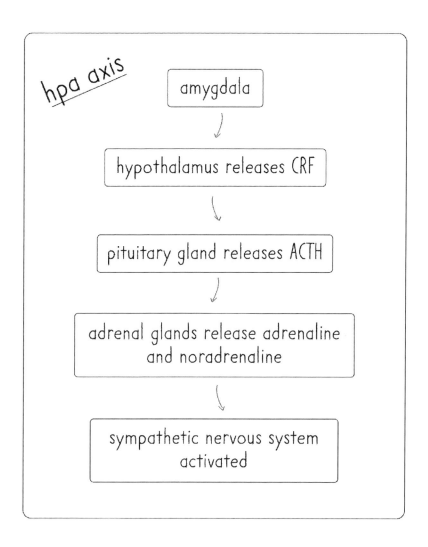

If our stress response is still activated after 30 minutes, we start releasing the stress-hormone cortisol, which then further activates our amygdala. This whole system is referred to as our hypothalamic pituitary adrenal (HPA) axis.

We all differ in our individual responses to stress. As mentioned, some of us may have higher levels of what psychologists call stress reactivity. People with high levels of stress reactivity may release more stress hormones, have a stronger sympathetic nervous system reaction, experience higher blood pressure, and/or have a higher heart rate during their stress response.

What are the possible causes of high stress reactivity? Past experiences of physical, sexual or emotional abuse, being bullied, experiencing stigma and/or discrimination, having parents or caregivers who don't treat you warmly, or having overprotective parents can all contribute to stress reactivity. As we've heard, Polly had a parent who didn't treat her warmly in childhood. She experienced a lot of stress and fear, which meant her amygdala repeatedly generated her stress response. This may have increased the overall activity of her amygdala, and thus her vulnerability to autostress as an adult. Our amygdala is like a muscle—the more it's used, the bigger and stronger it gets.

This would have made sense in terms of our survival for our ancient ancestors—the more they experienced fear, the more likely it is that they lived in a dangerous environment, and the more important it was for their brains to be able to sense and respond to danger.

Research has also found that a variation in the *serotonin transporter gene* is associated with amygdala overactivity. In every gene, we have two alleles, which can either be short or long. People with one or two copies of the *short allele* in the serotonin transporter gene have been found to have increased activity in the amygdala. Another variation in the *alpha2-adrenergic receptor gene* has also been linked to stronger sympathetic nervous system responses.

In addition to a possible genetic vulnerability and past experiences leading to high levels of stress reactivity, here's a diagram including everything else I've outlined that likely contributed to Polly's mental unwellness:

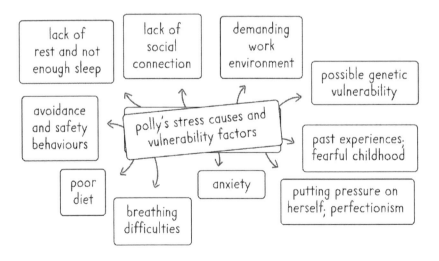

We can see how common experiences such as these can easily add up to create the high level of mental unwellness we see in society today. I've included a sample of The Stress Workbook at the end of this book to help you understand your experience better. When reflecting on possible reasons for mental unwellness, be mindful that there are likely numerous factors involved. This is normal, and it means that there are plenty of avenues to create positive change.

Here are 11 things I've described in The Framework that are thought to help us calm down the amygdala:

1. Learning to accept our body's stress response rather than fearing it.
2. Focusing on the benefits of stress.
3. Focusing on the meaning of stress.
4. Focusing on 'getting excited'.
5. Learning to overcome perfectionism and putting too much pressure on ourselves.
6. Breaking down tasks into smaller steps and using productivity tools to prevent ourselves from feeling overwhelmed.
7. Using cognitive defusion techniques, such as thinking of our thoughts as 'brain noise', telling ourselves 'I'm having the thought that' before our thoughts, or imagining them being said in a silly voice.
8. Using cognitive restructuring techniques such as the BOP method, focusing on balanced, optimistic and proactive thoughts.
9. Practising cognitive distraction.
10. Overcoming avoidance and reducing our safety behaviours.
11. Meeting our basic needs of getting enough rest, exercise, social connection, and proper nutrition.

bonus cat

Safety Meditation

Meditation, in a nutshell, is training the brain to focus on the here and now by directing our attention towards a sensory anchor (such as the breath, sounds, and bodily sensations). When we notice our minds wandering, we keep redirecting our attention to our sensory anchor in a non-judgmental way, with compassion and curiosity.

As we've heard, our mind can also be thought of as a sense. Focusing on thoughts (also called 'mantras') is another popular way to meditate.

After experimenting with different types of meditations, Polly tried making up her own mantras and found one theme in particular to be the most powerful: safety.

When using safety mantras, she noticed her body entered the relaxation state more often, and quicker. She realised that this made a lot of sense in terms of what she'd been learning about the amygdala.

You might want to experiment with your own mantras, but here are some suggestions:

- I trust the process,

- I am safe,
- I am safe, loved and worthy,
- I trust the nature of uncertainty,
- I trust the nature of change,
- All is well.

You could also experiment with repeating a single word you feel is soothing, such as calm, peace, or serenity.

6.2: Calming the Sympathetic Nervous System

"Almost everything will work again if you unplug it for a few minutes, including you." – Anne Lamott.

Sometimes it's hard to practise the techniques we listed that calm our amygdala as we may be going through a very difficult time in our lives. Our stress might lack meaning, be uncontrollable and be unpredictable. We might be experiencing financial difficulties, housing issues, or work-related issues—situations where it's hard to turn down our inner 'danger' signals. In these cases, we could enter a state of autostress, where we have ongoing stress symptoms. When this happens, we can try our best to calm our sympathetic nervous system.

Our sympathetic nervous system (SNS) is part of our autonomic nervous system (ANS), the part of our body responsible for controlling and regulating life-sustaining functions you don't have to think about. It's our ANS that keeps us alive when we're asleep or when we get knocked unconscious. It controls bodily functions such as breathing, blood pressure, our heartbeat, and digestive processes.

Our ANS consists of the SNS and the parasympathetic nervous system (PNS). Our SNS is involved in creating the stress response, whereas the PNS is involved in the relaxation response, allowing us to 'rest and digest'.

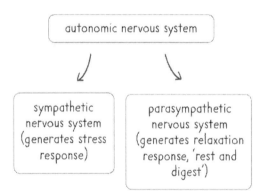

When we're autostressed, our sympathetic nervous system goes into overdrive and it gives rise to the varied distressing physical reactions. Making efforts to balance the activity of our ANS helps us feel more at ease. For example, when it comes to our digestive system, our SNS reduces salivation and peristalsis (the process of food moving through the digestive system), which can lead to IBS symptoms associated with stress. On the other hand, our PNS stimulates salivation and peristalsis, which can ease IBS symptoms. We balance the ANS by activating our PNS. The relaxation response is a term coined by Dr Herbert Benson in 1975. He discovered the response in the same room at Harvard University that the fight-or-flight stress response was discovered! He explains:

> *"When you elicit the relaxation response, your energy usage is lowered, your heart beats slower, your muscles relax and your blood pressure decreases. If practiced regularly, it can have lasting effects."* He notes, *"anything that breaks the train of everyday thought will evoke this physiological state."*

Activating Our Parasympathetic Nervous System

Here's 4 things we've covered in The Framework that are thought to activate our PNS:

1. Practising Relaxation

Not surprisingly, practising relaxation is top of the list! Research suggests this is very powerful. In 2008, Benson and colleagues led a study that found that long-term practice of the relaxation response even changes the expression of our genes in a way which makes us more resilient to stress and anxiety. Here's a recap of some things we can do to achieve a state of relaxation, as described in section 5.2:

- Progressive muscle relaxation,
- Visualisation,
- Yoga,
- Pilates,
- Tai Chi,
- Massages,
- Gentle stretching,
- Spending time in nature,
- Mindful colouring,
- Listening to music,
- Warm baths,
- Playing a musical instrument,
- A creative activity (such as drawing and painting),
- Floatation therapy,
- Doing a digital detox.

2. Practising Deep Breathing

Practising slow, deep breathing is thought to activate the PNS. As Dr John Arden (who coined the term 'autostress') explains:

> *"Your breathing and heart rate are interconnected. As you learn to breathe more deeply,*

your heart rate will slow, and you can enjoy a calm and clear frame of mind."

As we outlined in section 5.2, breathing difficulties are the root cause of many stress symptoms: shortness of breath, chest tightness, tingling or numbness in the arms, fingers, toes, or around the mouth, feeling dizzy and light-headed, weakness, heart pounding, racing and palpitations, sweating or hot flushes, headaches, feeling sick and fatigue. Committing to practising deep breathing on a regular basis can therefore be an effective way to help ourselves feel better.

3. Practising Mindfulness and Meditation

Dr Herbert Benson discovered the relaxation response when examining people who practised Transcendental Meditation. This involves sitting with our eyes closed and focusing our attention on a particular mantra (as described in the Safety Meditation). He found that while people meditated, their breathing slowed, and levels of blood lactate (a chemical in our bodies that's associated with stress and anxiety) decreased. There's now an abundance of research showing that mindfulness and meditation practise can effectively reduce stress, autostress, and anxiety.

What makes the simple practise of mindfulness and meditation so powerful is their wide-reaching effects. They essentially makes our minds, brains and bodies less reactive to stress and anxiety through several different mechanisms. For example, they help us develop awareness of our physical reactions, so we can relax our muscles when we notice they're tense. We get better at noticing negative thoughts and unhelpful thinking patterns without getting carried away by them—we can better prevent ourselves from reaching the bottom of the Slide of Doom! Other proven benefits include enhancing our self-compassion, improving our concentration, creativity, and more.

be here meow

4. Practising The Two Arrows of Happiness Mindset

People who experience more positive emotions have been found to have higher parasympathetic nervous system activity, lower blood pressure and reduced levels of stress hormones such as cortisol. We also heard in section 5.5 about how positive emotions and positive social connections are associated with increased activity in our vagus nerve, part of our PNS. Research suggests that people who experience more positive emotions such as gratitude are quicker at returning to a normal state after experiencing the stress response, meaning their bodies are more resilient to stress.

bonus cat

Animal Therapy

Research suggests that animals can help us reduce our stress response by lowering our blood pressure. A study by Dr Adnan Qureshi found that in a sample of 4,435 people, over a 10 year follow up period, people who owned a cat showed a 30% lower risk of death from heart attack compared to non-cat owners.

There are a few theories as to why animal therapy is effective. One is the biophilia hypothesis—essentially that humans have an innate propensity to connect with other living things—which explains why walks in the park (a.k.a. 'ecotherapy') can be so therapeutic! Another theory is that spending time with animals is essentially a mindfulness exercise. It gives us a break from focusing on our negative thoughts and worries, and we're more in the present moment. (Plus, it might have something to do with the unconditional love they give us!).

If you can't have a pet because your landlord won't allow it, you could always embrace digital pet therapy. That's right—research by Jessica Myrick at Indiana University found that watching cat videos online is enough to boost positive emotions and even energy. She also found that people reported fewer negative emotions, such as anxiety, annoyance and sadness, after watching cats online.

6.3: Calming the Right Prefrontal Cortex

"Great things are done by a series of small things brought together." – Vincent Van Gough.

We've just learnt which actions are helping us calm down our amygdala and sympathetic nervous system, helping us to reduce and transform stress, autostress and anxiety.

There's one last important shift that's happening when we start feeling calmer and happier—the shift from the right prefrontal cortex (R-PFC) to the left prefrontal cortex (L-PFC). The ratio of activity between these is our happiness level set point.

Our brain consists of two cerebral hemispheres—the left and right hemispheres—and four lobes, the frontal lobe, parietal lobe, occipital lobe, and temporal lobe. The prefrontal cortex is a part of our brain located at the front of the frontal lobe.

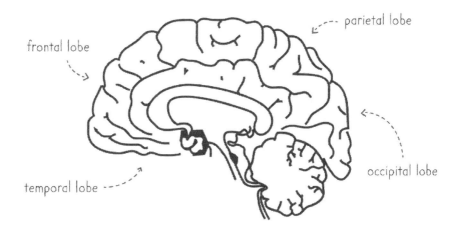

In general, more activation of the L-PFC is associated with good mood, whilst the R-PFC is associated with low mood, anxiety and being easily upset.

The R-PFC is also associated with avoidance whereas the L-PFC is associated with 'approach' behaviours—facing our fears and stepping out of our comfort zones.

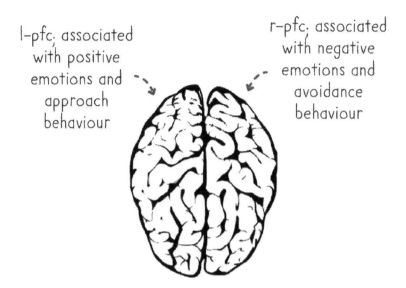

l-pfc: associated with positive emotions and approach behaviour

r-pfc: associated with negative emotions and avoidance behaviour

This means that the more we avoid what makes us anxious, the more anxious and down we'll feel, as we're activating the already overactive right prefrontal cortex which is associated with negative emotions.

This is why it's so important to push ourselves out of our comfort zones and tackle the things we're avoiding. Every time we face our fears and practice our mental wellness skills, we activate the L-PFC, which is associated with good mood. This helps shift our happiness level set point.

The more we use our L-PFC, the stronger its connections become, and the easier it gets for us dampen overactivity of our amygdala and R-PFC. In other words, the more we practice our mental wellness skills and stepping outside of our comfort zones, the easier it gets. This is because 'cells that fire together, wire together'.

Remember the quote from Dr Rick Hanson in 4.1?

> "By taking just a few extra seconds to stay with a positive experience—even the comfort in a single breath—you'll help turn a passing mental state into lasting neural structure."

The more we practice happiness, the easier it gets for our brains to experience that state. Eventually, we'll have shifted our happiness level set point, rewiring our brains in a way that gives rise to a stable sense of contentment.

This is called neuroplasticity, the ability of our brain to literally rewire itself. We use our minds to change our brain.

We might be born with a vulnerability towards stress, autostress and anxiety. We may endure life experiences that make our stress response strong and unpredictable. We may have inherited unhelpful thinking patterns from our parents, caregivers or peers. But we all have the ability to help ourselves feel better.

In The Framework, I've described the numerous small steps we can make that together, create big change. Here's an overview of the gradual steps Polly has made over the past two years:

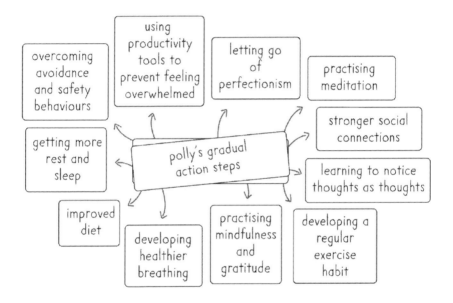

When it comes to pieces of advice, I'll save the best 'til last: be kind to yourself.

I hope this book has given you more clarity around your mental health, which will allow you to be more understanding and kinder to yourself.

Finally, I wish you the very best on your journey towards a calmer, happier you.

"It does not matter how slowly you go, as long as you do not stop." – Confucius.

Why not think of a small step you can take today?

A Final Word

Congratulations on finishing The Framework! You've just digested a lot of information—please keep in mind this book is designed to be read and reread on a regular basis for maximum impact.

I recommend you set yourself a challenge to read The Framework once a month, taking notes and planning small steps for six months if you're serious about creating positive change!

A lot of Polly's story is based on my own. There are elements too personal to include here, but I hope that Polly's/my story will resonate with others.

I'm particularly passionate about raising awareness of the concepts of autostress and high stress reactivity as this is what I most identify with. I feel that our current conception of anxiety places too much emphasis on the mind-based elements rather than the body-based elements. This lack of differentiation between the two may be leaving people feeling confused about their experience and even somewhat blamed for not being able to reduce it with the likes of cognitive techniques. To me, the terms autostress and stress reactivity yield more understanding, more compassion, and a clearer path forward in terms of feeling better.

I'm also incredibly passionate about happiness. I was once so cynical about it that I even wrote an article 'Why You Should Stop Pursuing Happiness' on the website Thought Catalogue! I'd honestly never experienced a stable good mood before. I had a resting bitch face, and now I often have a resting smile face—I know the Two Arrows of Happiness concept works!

To support you to create real positive change, I've created The Workbook. Whereas The Framework is primarily designed to help you *understand* your mental wellness, The Workbook is designed to help you *enhance* your mental wellness. Using a practical, action-oriented approach, you can plan your gradual action steps to becoming your calmer, happier self. Head to www.thewellnesssociety.org to check it out!

If you've found this book useful and think others would benefit from it too, please, please, please could you leave short review on Amazon? This really helps the book reach a wider audience (Amazon will rank it further up the search listings)!

And if you're interested in getting involved and following the journey, please find me on social media: Instagram: @thewellnesssocietyorg, Pinterest: TheWellnessSociety.

With love,

Becca
x

The Stress and Autostress Workbook Text Sample
(Available from www.thewellnesssociety.org)

Here are some common stress triggers and vulnerability factors. Tick the ones you currently identify with:

☐ **Past experiences** – physical, sexual or emotional abuse, bullying, experiencing stigma and/or discrimination, having parents or caregivers who don't treat you warmly, or having overprotective parents can all contribute to stress reactivity.

☐ **Culture of danger and threat** – growing up or socialising with people who are preoccupied with danger and threat or have unhelpful beliefs and/or thinking patterns may mean you're more likely to be develop the same things.

☐ **Possible genetic vulnerability** – having a family history of high stress reactivity and anxiety might mean we've inherited genes that mean we're more likely to have high stress reactivity and anxiety.

☐ **Breathing difficulties** – when we get into the habit of shallow or over-breathing we risk experiencing a range of physical symptoms, including: chest tightness, breathing difficulties, a rapid heartbeat, dizziness, numbness and tingling, and a sense that the self and/or the world isn't real.

☐ **Feeling overwhelmed** – when we feel like our demands outweigh our resources, and we're under too much pressure (including putting pressure on ourselves).

☐ **Facing big life changes** – when we're experiencing big, meaningful life changes such as moving house, starting a new job or coming out of a long-term relationship.

☐ **Having little control over something we care about** – for example, awaiting the decision of an important interview, or dealing with personal illness or the illness of a loved one.

☐ **Facing challenges often** – when something relates to our personal values and has an uncertain outcome (such as an exam, public speaking, or a social interaction), we may trigger our stress response.

☐ **Anxiety** – fearing our body's stress response and focusing on and exaggerating the negatives of situations are all examples of how anxiety can trigger and intensify our stress response, creating the stress-anxiety loop of escalating stress and anxiety.

☐ **Unhelpful core beliefs** – for example, the belief that we need everyone's social approval, that we must never make mistakes, or that we're not good enough can cause anxiety that triggers our stress response.

☐ **Not meeting our basic needs** – when we're not getting enough rest and sleep (for example, due to long working hours), feel socially isolated and/or have a poor diet, we risk triggering our body's stress response.

☐ **Using safety behaviours and avoidance** – these alleviate stress in the short-term, but prolong it in the long run.

☐ **Not having enough to do** – this can trigger the stress response just as much as having too much to do!

It's likely you have a variety of personal stress triggers and vulnerability factors. Try not to feel overwhelmed by this. It is normal. There's lots of possible ways to transform and reduce stress! Plus, alleviating stress and autostress isn't best seen as a goal, it's more like an ongoing life mission! The good news is, when we become more familiar with our triggers and our physical reactions, we can take quicker and more effective action to help ourselves feel better.

This becomes a self-awareness loop: when we become more aware of our triggers, we become more aware of our physical reactions, when we become more aware of our physical reactions, we become more aware of our triggers.

Review the common stress triggers and vulnerability factors on the previous page. Write these in the diagram below along with any others you can think of, and make a note of which category they fall into: accept, transform or reduce.

References

Ahmed, I. (2014). *Triumphs of Experience: The Men of the Harvard Grant Study.*

Arden, J. (2014). *Brain Based Therapy for Anxiety: A Workbook for Clinicians and Clients.* PESI Publishing & Media.

Arden, J. B. (2015*). Brain2Brain: Enacting Client Change Through the Persuasive Power of Neuroscience.* John Wiley & Sons.

Ben Congleton Tweet:
https://twitter.com/madalynrose/status/880886024725024769?lang=en

Blascovich, J., & Tomaka, J. (1996). The biopsychosocial model of arousal regulation. Advances in Experimental Social Psychology, 28, 1–51.

Brehm, J. W., & Cohen, A. R. (1962). Explorations in cognitive dissonance.

Brooks, A. W. (2014). Get excited: Reappraising pre-performance anxiety as excitement. Journal of Experimental Psychology: General, 143, 1144–1158.

Brotheridge, C. (2017). *The Anxiety Solution: A Quieter Mind, a Calmer You.* Penguin Books.

Cacioppo, J. T. (1998). Somatic responses to psychological stress: The reactivity hypothesis.

Carr, A. (2012). *Clinical psychology: An introduction.* Routledge.

Catalino, L. I., Algoe, S. B., & Fredrickson, B. L. (2014). Prioritizing positivity: An effective approach to pursuing happiness?. Emotion, 14(6), 1155.

Chloe McLeod Quote:
http://www.huffingtonpost.com.au/2016/03/16/macronutrient-balanced-meals_n_9466284.html.

Cooper, C. L., & Quick, J. C. (Eds.). (2017). *The Handbook of Stress and Health: A Guide to Research and Practice.* John Wiley & Sons.

Creswell, J. D., Welch, W. T., Taylor, S. E., Sherman, D. K., Gruenewald, T. L., & Mann, T. (2005). Affirmation of personal values buffers neuroendocrine and psychological stress responses. Psychological Science, 16, 846-851.

Crum, A. J., Salovey, P., & Achor, S. (2013). Rethinking stress: The role of mindsets in determining the stress response. Journal of Personality and Social Psychology, 104, 716.

Dienstbier, R. A. (1989). Arousal and physiological toughness: implications for mental and physical health. Psychological review, 96(1), 84.

Dusek, J. A., Otu, H. H., Wohlhueter, A. L., Bhasin, M., Zerbini, L. F., Joseph, M. G., ... & Libermann, T. A. (2008). Genomic counter-stress changes induced by the relaxation response. PloS one, 3(7), e2576.

Ebner, K., & Singewald, N. (2017). Individual differences in stress susceptibility and stress inhibitory mechanisms. Current Opinion in Behavioral Sciences, 14, 54-64.

Evans, J. (2013). Philosophy for Life and Other Dangerous Situations: Ancient Philosophy for Modern Problems. New World Library.

Hanson, R. (2013). Hardwiring Happiness: The Practical Science of Reshaping Your Brain-and Your Life. Random House.

Harris, R. (2008). The Happiness Trap. London: Constable & Robinson Ltd.

Herbert Benson Quote: https://www.bensonhenryinstitute.org/2017/03/17/study-finds-relaxation-response-triggers-genomic-changes/ and http://www.apa.org/monitor/2008/10/relaxation.aspx

Hölzel, B. K., Lazar, S. W., Gard, T., Schuman-Olivier, Z., Vago, D. R., & Ott, U. (2011). How does mindfulness meditation work? Proposing mechanisms of action from a conceptual and neural perspective. Perspectives on psychological science, 6(6), 537-559.

Knight, S. (2015). The Life-Changing Magic of Not Giving a F**k: The bestselling book everyone is talking about (A No F*cks Given Guide). Quercus.

Kok, B. E., Coffey, K. A., Cohn, M. A., Catalino, L. I., Vacharkulksemsuk, T., Algoe, S. B., ... & Fredrickson, B. L. (2013). How positive emotions build physical health: Perceived positive social connections account for the upward spiral between positive emotions and vagal tone. Psychological science, 24(7), 1123-1132.

Lahnna Catalino Quote: https://greatergood.berkeley.edu/article/item/a_better_way_to_pursue_happiness

Littlehales, N. (2016). *Sleep: Redefine Your Rest, for Success in Work, Sport and Life.* Penguin Books.

Loprinzi, P. D., & Cardinal, B. J. (2011). Association between objectively-measured physical activity and sleep, NHANES 2005–2006. Mental Health and Physical Activity, 4(2), 65-69.

McGonigal, K. (2015). *The upside of stress: Why stress is good for you, and how to get good at it.* New York, NY: Penguin.

Mental Health Foundation Report:
https://www.mentalhealth.org.uk/publications/surviving-or-thriving-state-uks-mental-health

Mental Health Foundation Social Connection Report:
https://www.mentalhealth.org.uk/publications/relationships-21st-century-forgotten-foundation-mental-health-and-wellbeing

Mikkelsen, K., Stojanovska, L., Polenakovic, M., Bosevski, M., & Apostolopoulos, V. (2017). Exercise and mental health. Maturitas.

Myles, P., & Shafran, R. (2015). *The CBT Handbook: A comprehensive guide to using Cognitive Behavioural Therapy to overcome depression, anxiety and anger.* Hachette UK.

Myrick, J. G. (2015). Emotion regulation, procrastination, and watching cat videos online: Who watches Internet cats, why, and to what effect?. *Computers in Human Behavior, 52,* 168-176.

Nancy Etcoff TED Talk:
https://www.ted.com/talks/nancy_etcoff_on_happiness_and_why_we_want_it

NHS Sleep Quote: https://www.nhs.uk/Livewell/tiredness-and-fatigue/Pages/lack-of-sleep-health-risks.aspx

Nicky Lidbetter quote: http://www.redonline.co.uk/health-self/self/how-to-recognise-high-functioning-anxiety

Oriach, C. S., Robertson, R. C., Stanton, C., Cryan, J. F., & Dinan, T. G. (2016). Food for thought: The role of nutrition in the microbiota-gut–brain axis. *Clinical Nutrition Experimental, 6,* 25-38.

Petruzzello, S. J., Landers, D. M., Hatfield, B. D., Kubitz, K. A., & Salazar, W. (1991). A meta-analysis on the anxiety-reducing effects of acute and chronic exercise. Sports medicine, 11(3), 143-182.

Pittman, C. M., & Karle, E. M. (2015). Rewire Your Anxious Brain: How to Use the Neuroscience of Fear to End Anxiety, Panic, and Worry. New Harbinger Publications.

Premenstrual Syndrome Information: https://www.nhs.uk/conditions/pre-menstrual-syndrome/

Qureshi, A. I., Memon, M. Z., Vazquez, G., & Suri, M. F. K. (2009). Cat ownership and the Risk of Fatal Cardiovascular Diseases. Results from the Second National Health and Nutrition Examination Study Mortality Follow-up Study. *Journal of vascular and interventional neurology*, *2*(1), 132.

Rada, P., Avena, N. M., & Hoebel, B. G. (2005). Daily bingeing on sugar repeatedly releases dopamine in the accumbens shell. *Neuroscience*, *134*(3), 737-744.

Robert Waldinger Quote: https://news.harvard.edu/gazette/story/2017/04/over-nearly-80-years-harvard-study-has-been-showing-how-to-live-a-healthy-and-happy-life/

Sarah Knight Quote: https://www.theguardian.com/lifeandstyle/2016/jan/01/drowning-commitments-stop-giving-a-damn-sarah-knight

Seery, M. D. (2013). The biopsychosocial model of challenge and threat: Using the heart to measure the mind. *Social and Personality Psychology Compass*, *7*(9), 637-653.

Shim, S., Crum, A., & Galinsky, A. D. (in press). The Grace of Control: How A Can-Control Mindset Increases Health, Performance, and Well-being.

The Food and Mood Project Survey: http://www.comfirst.org.uk/files/food_mood_survey_summary.pdf

Wiseman, R. (2014). *Night School: Wake up to the power of sleep*. Pan Macmillan.

Printed in Great Britain
by Amazon